WHAT A DIRTY SHAME!

101 Unforgettable Place Names of
Oklahoma

By Jim Marion Etter

NEW FORUMS PRESS INC.

Published in the United States of America
by New Forums Press, Inc. 1018 S. Lewis St.
Stillwater, OK 74074
www.newforums.com

Copyright © 2010 by New Forums Press, Inc.

This title was originally published in 2007 during Oklahoma's Centennial celebration as *What a Dirty Shame! 100 Unforgettable Place Names of Oklahoma.* A new chapter has been added for this edition of the work.

All rights reserved. No part of this publication may be reproduced or transmitted in any form or by any means, electronic or mechanical, including photocopy, or any information storage or retrieval system, without permission in writing from the publisher.

Library of Congress Cataloging-in-Publication Data Pending

This book may be ordered in bulk quantities at discount from New Forums Press, Inc., P.O. Box 876, Stillwater, OK 74076 [Federal I.D. No. 73 1123239]. Printed in the United States of America.

International Standard Book Number: 1-58107-173-6

To everyone who has ever driven along some Oklahoma road and said "There must be a story behind a name like that!"

Contents

Foreword ix

Acknowledgements x

What a Dirty Shame! 100 Unforgettable Place Names
of Oklahoma 1

Spiro Mounds (circa 950 A.D.) – Long, Long Ago 2

Devil's Canyon (circa 1611) – *'Cañón del Diablo'* 4

Cimarron River (circa 1650) — A Pot of Beans 7

Ferdinandina (circa 1719) – A Royal 'Mess' 10

San Bernardo (1759) – The Wichitas 12

Navajoe (circa 1760) – The Comanches 15

Rainy Mountain (circa 1797) – The Kiowas 19

Sequoyah (circa 1829) – The Cherokees 22

Wigwam Neosho (circa 1829) – Sam Houston 24

Eagle Town (circa 1832) — The Choctaws 26

Cutthroat Gap (circa 1833) – A Sad 'Presence' 28

Boggy Depot (1837) – 'On the Boggy' 30

Going Snake (circa 1839) – A Memorable Name 32

Antelope Hills (circa 1849) – Animals, Art and Stories 34

Packsaddle Crossing (circa 1858) – A Span of Theories 37

Tamaha (1864) – The Steamboat 40

Camp Napoleon (1865) – Big Powwow 42

Robbers' Roost (1867) – 'Blast 'em Out!' 44

Ghost Mound (circa 1867) – The Rise of Legends 46

Left Hand Spring (1868) – The Chisholm Trail 48

Ghost Hollow (circa 1871) – Spooks and Gun Smoke 52

Cowboy Hill (circa 1871) – The Great 101 54
Glass Mountains (1873) – 'Glassy' or 'Glossy' 59
Polecat Station (circa 1873) – Stages, Not Skunks 61
Hennessey (1874) – The Ambush 62
Doan's Crossing (1874) – The Great Western 65
Needmore (circa 1875) – Not Short of Memories 67
Trail (circa 1875) – Horses and Trains 69
Sacred Heart (circa 1875) – A Mission and Mystery Books 71
Wauhillau (circa 1879) – Ned and a Water Mill 73
Robbers Cave (circa 1880) – Belle's Abode? 74
Oklahoma (1881) — An OK Idea! 76
Wetumka (1881) — A Bunch of Suckers 78
Dead Indian Lake (circa 1881) – Non-politically Right 80
Paw Paw (1882) – 'Way Down Yonder ...' 82
Tin City (circa 1883) – Prairie Patchwork 83
Keokuk Falls (circa 1888) – Jim Thorpe 85
Beer City (circa 1888) – A State Line Tradition 87
Nowata (1889) – A Dry Place? 89
Corner (circa 1889) – 'Bootlegger' and Four Nooses 91
Loco (1890) – A Town with Savvy 93
Okarche (1890) – 'Bless you!' 95
Eldorado (1890) – 'All That Glisters ...' 97
Hope (1890) – Still Plenty of It 99
Fairmount Cemetery (circa 1890) – A Good Horse 101
Oologah (circa 1890) – 'Will' 103
Spook Light Road (circa 1890) – 'Looking For His Head' 105
Chickiechockie (1891) – Chickie and Reba 107
Grand (1892) – A Fine Mystery 109

Dogtown (circa 1892) – Howlin' Days of Summer 111
Horsethief Canyon (circa 1892) – A Catchy Name 113
Buzzards' Roost (circa 1892) – Jesse James? 115
Okeene (circa 1892) – Snakes Alive! 117
Saddle Mountain (circa 1893) – The Peak of Nostalgia 119
Lost City (circa 1893) – Found by a Star 121
Geronimo (1894) – A Warrior 123
Moscow Flats (1894) – Pure Americana 125
Violet Springs (circa 1894) – No Flowers 126
Kansas (circa 1894) – The Little One 128
Mustang (circa 1894) – Horses and High Class 130
Sulphur (1895) – Name with a Smell 132
Maud and Bowlegs (1896 and 1927) – Not Very Nice 134
Berlin (circa 1896) – Luck of the Draw 136
Wildcat (1897) – More Like a Kitten? 138
Frogville (1897) – River Serenades 140
Wildman (1900) – Mining Mayhem 141
Big Pasture (circa 1900) – Texas Cattle and Wolves 143
Gotebo (circa 1900) – A Popular Guy 146
Nofire Hollow (circa 1900) – Wes Lived There 149
Punkin Ridge (circa 1900) – Watermelons, Too 151
Roman Nose (circa 1900) – Name with a Face 154
Texhoma (circa 1901) – A Pair of States 156
Starvation Creek (circa 1901) – Tough Times? 158
Hooker (1902) – Not Really 160
Dempsey (1903) – Oklahoma Weather 162
America (1903) – More Than a Name 165
Bugtussle (1903) – 'Little Giant' 167

Okesa (circa 1905) – Unforgettable Elmer 168

Vamoosa (1906) – 'That Name Will Do!' 170

Saint Louis (circa 1906) – Joking Around 172

Wild Horse Mountain (circa 1906) – Barbecue Country 174

Moonshine Road (circa 1907) – Spirited Memories 176

Medicine Spring (circa 1909) – Gilbert's 'Hidalgo' 178

Strong City (circa 1911) – Firewater Express 180

Ragtown (1913) – Tents, Shacks and Peddlers 182

Titanic (circa 1915) – Unsinkable? 183

Salt Springs (1920) – Racing for Dollars 185

Babbs Switch (circa 1920) – A Christmas Tragedy 187

Pie Flat (circa 1920) – Sweet Things 190

Wizzbang (1921) – Boomtown 191

Tater Hill (circa 1924) – Dizzy Dean 193

Dirty Shame (circa 1925) – A Lovely Landmark 195

Ticky Ridge (circa 1925) – Itchy Subjects 198

Cross Bell Ranch (circa 1927) – Trouble in the Osage 200

Slapout (1932) – A Small Inventory 203

Possum Hollow (circa 1934) – 'A Way of Life' 205

Tia Juana (circa 1938) – North of the Border 207

Gene Autry (1941) – A Magic Name 209

Red Rock Canyon (1956) – Unique, Sorta 212

Lottawatta Road (circa 1964) – A Way of Talkin' 214

Nowhere (circa 1976) – Definitely There 216

Afterword 218

Index 219

Foreword

There is probably not an Oklahoman or a visitor to Oklahoma who hasn't wondered about the meaning or origin of the names of many of our cities and towns and other landmarks.

Those names mirror the 46th state's diverse culture and unique history. They sing with the beauty of American Indian languages, reflect the hope or earthy humor of early settlers, or ring with the energy of entrepreneurs.

In some instances, the record documenting the birth of an Oklahoma place name no longer exists – if it ever did. In others, the "official" version varies from local legend – or is greatly enlivened by it!

Respected Oklahoma author Jim Etter examines both history and folklore – and that intriguing blend of both – in this work that results from his years as a journalist whose work has taken him to hundreds of Oklahoma communities where he talked with – and listened to – thousands of Oklahomans.

The result is a book that is both informative and entertaining and quintessentially Oklahoman – part fact, part fiction and bigger and better than either.

J. Blake Wade, Executive Director
Oklahoma Centennial Commemoration
Commission

Acknowledgements

The author truly appreciates the help of sources including Bob Blackburn, executive director of the Oklahoma Historical Society, as well as OHS staff members Michael Dean, Whit Edwards, Larry O'Dell, Edward Connie Shoemaker, Mary Jane Warde and Bill Welge; Donald DeWitt, curator of Western History Collections, University of Oklahoma; Kaye Bond, curator of the Cherokee Strip Museum at Perry; Glen McIntyre, curator of the Museum of the Cherokee Strip at Enid; Gary Ray Howell and Thom Renbarger, both of the Oklahoma Department of Transportation; T. Wayne Furr, executive secretary of the Oklahoma Board on Geographic Names; Alecia Gonzales of Anadarko, Kiowa language teacher; Jim Argo and David McDaniel, who as photographers for *The Daily Oklahoman* helped the author seek out nearly forgotten places throughout the state; John W. Morris, Charles R. Goins and the late Edwin C. McReynolds, authors of "Historical Atlas of Oklahoma"; the late W.S. Nye, historical writer of Fort Sill and Plains Indians; the late Ken Turner, director of the No Man's Land Museum in Goodwell; the late Kent Ruth, Oklahoma historian and travel writer; the late Phil Harris, historical columnist for *The Muskogee Daily Phoenix & Times-Democrat;* the late George Shirk, author of "Oklahoma Place Names"; several librarians throughout the state; as well as various historians listed elsewhere in this book.

The author also wants to thank a whole bunch of good ol' boys and nice gals for their precious memories and comments.

WHAT A DIRTY SHAME!

101 Unforgettable Place Names of Oklahoma

Oklahomans put a lot of stock in words that describe their places. And they love to hear the story about the place.

They have a yen for both talking and hearing about the Sooner State's many American Indian names; others spiced with Spanish; those about cattle trails and the Old West, historic battles, early oil wells and boomtowns, and the "Okies" who rattled westward on Route 66 during the days of the Great Depression and Dust Bowl.

The same goes for sites of bloodshed and other tragedies; along with the state's odious background of land stealers, gunslingers, horse thieves, illegal whiskey peddlers, crooked politicians and other scamps.

It is difficult to fully record all of this in a single book – and maybe even harder for one book to cover all the state's places that are interesting to everyone.

However, in this book, which is an expanded version of my first "WHAT A DIRTY SHAME," written for the state's centennial, I have tried to briefly portray both the history and culture of Oklahoma by describing 101 places that I consider unforgettable.

Here's hoping I have done that.

The Author
www.jimetter.com

Spiro Mounds (circa 950 A.D.) – Long, Long Ago

The place that came to be called Spiro Mounds, near the present-day town of Spiro, in LeFlore County of eastern Oklahoma, represents a culture that existed long before there was an "Oklahoma," or even "Indian Territory" – and even before human beings like the ones who lived there came to be called American Indians.

It existed so far back in time, many scholars won't speculate what the surrounding region during that period could be called, if anything.

The mounds – 12 of them in an area of 150 acres – are considered evidence of agriculture and other aspects of an advanced civilization dating back to between 850 A.D. and 1450 A.D.

It's believed that the people of that time and place farmed and engaged in commerce, and that their descendants finally came to be known as both the Indian tribes of Caddo and Wichita. Historians have said the mounds comprise "one of the four most important prehistoric Indian sites east of the Rocky Mountains."

As to the town of Spiro, it apparently was settled in the late 1890s in the Choctaw Nation of Indian Territory, its post office opening on Sept. 21, 1898. The name may have come from Spiro Nicodemus, wife of an early-day resident.

"Spiro" was then used to designate the nearby site of the mounds, as the Spiro Mounds Archaeological State Park, in the 1930s. The site, operated by the Oklahoma Historical Society, became the Spiro Mounds Archaeological Center in 1978.

Nearly 1,057 years after the ancient occupation of the Mounds region, the Spiro Mounds center was a popular historical attraction for some 12,000 visitors a year, according to Dennis Peterson, the center's curator.

And, Harold Gist of Sallisaw, a retired government worker in his early 70s who said he grew up "around the mounds," recalled when people "used to go in there and dig at their own will – for pottery, arrow heads and what have you."

He also spoke of "a little one-room log post office" that was called Mounds – as well as when "Spiro was a very nice little place, back when we had cotton."

But the roads, he said, weren't good during wet weather. "We'd go to town in a wagon and team, and the roads to Spiro were bad when it was muddy – I remember those old mules slippin' and slidin'."

Even worse, he says, was a time when Spiro "had a bad problem" with its sewage disposal — "if you got within four or five miles of town, you'd know it."

And that reminded him of a Spiro anecdote:

During World War II, a passenger train was approaching town, and before the conductor could walk through and call out the name of the next stop, a woman passenger changed her baby's diaper, then tossed it out an open window – or thought she did.

The diaper flew into the seat behind her, where a soldier was sitting.

"And according to the story," Gist said, "it hit the soldier boy in the face. And he jumped up and hollered 'Spiro!'"

Devil's Canyon (circa 1611) – 'Cañón del Diablo'

Devil's Canyon, near Lugert and Lake Altus-Lugert in present-day Kiowa County of southwestern Oklahoma, has a history dating back to the early 1600s when the region was claimed by Spain — and to an 1834 peace council in that part of Indian Territory believed to have been the first formal contact between the U.S. government and Plains Indians.

The canyon is also significant because it borders the sizeable corner of present-day Oklahoma — to the south and west of the North Fork of the Red River — that was part of Texas for more than three decades.

Following a period when its title was in dispute, that region in February 1860 officially became Greer County, Texas, but as result of a U.S. court ruling in March 1896 became part of Indian Territory, and in May the same year was attached to Oklahoma Territory.

While part of Texas, it encompassed the present-day Oklahoma counties of Greer, Harmon and Jackson and part of Beckham – and has come to be referred to ever since as "Old Greer County."

Regarding the 1834 meeting in the Devil's Canyon area, it involved a visit by the U.S. Dragoons from Fort Gibson in the eastern portion of the territory, to a large Wichita village — a camp that was described in a report by Lt. T.B. Wheelock of the Dragoons as consisting of "nearly 200 grass lodges."

It's believed the canyon, a rocky gap that opens toward the North Fork of the Red and is at the edge of the Quartz Mountains, was named by Spanish explorers, probably as *"Cañón del Diablo."*

It's also been surmised that the name, in English, was further affixed to the great gorge by members of the Dragoon expedition more than two centuries later – and before that, had long been repeated in the Wichita language, as stories from the Spanish had survived among the Indians.

Historical reports say a "Great Spanish Road to Red River" entered present-day Oklahoma near the North Fork, and that an "Old Spanish Town" was established in or near the canyon in the early 17th century. Some accounts say Spanish missionaries were there in 1611.

One report has it that a Texas geologist, sometime before 1896 when the region across the North Fork was still part of Texas, found the remains of a "Mexican village" near the mouth of the canyon.

The canyon, laying for more than a mile between peaks of granite, also carries legends of "lost Spanish mines," and hidden treasure, buried by Spaniards, bandits or raiding Indians.

The general area of the canyon was the site of a battle between U.S. soldiers and a band of Comanches and Kiowas in December of 1868 – a clash pretty much considered a draw.

The remote place has also been called "Haunted Canyon," because of the many stories told about it over the years, inspired by reports of ruins of structures, Indian relics and especially bones – even an entire skeleton – having been found there.

Among the oldest legends about the canyon has it that at some point during the history of the region, Kiowa Indians, upon discovering the Spanish village, where gold was being mined, killed and scalped the Spaniards and looted the place of some 50 burro loads of gold bullion.

The Indians hid the gold, the story goes, and never revealed where.

Some 395 years after the canyon's reported occupation by Spaniards, the ravine still appeared a rough and wild region amid brushy hills and not easily accessible for humans. The canyon itself was owned by the state's Quartz Mountain Resort Park, south of Lone Wolf, but enclosed by private property.

While the origin of "Devil's Canyon" wasn't documented, some local history enthusiasts had no doubt about it.

"The Spaniards have the name claim," said Susan Cabaniss Bradford of Duke, a teacher and veteran collector of southwestern Oklahoma lore.

She said the word *"Diablo"* definitely shows up in research of the canyon's history – and she theorized the Spaniards had a purpose behind the name.

"By telling the natives that it was 'a Devil's Canyon,' they could keep them away for a time," she said – at least, "until the Kiowa figured it out."

However, Sue Hokanson, a naturalist at the Quartz Mountain park, raised another possibility behind the "devil" part of the name.

"The thing I heard was that the wind whistled through it," she said, referring to the canyon's thick growth and jagged ridges, "and sounded like the howling of ghouls and demons."

Some observers had a simpler theory. They suggested the early occupants of the canyon – whoever they were – decided the rough terrain, summertime heat, rattlesnakes and insects made it "a hellish place!"

Cimarron River (circa 1650) – A Pot of Beans

The Cimarron River in present-day Oklahoma may have been unofficially named in the 1600s by hunters or stockmen in what was part of the vast country claimed by Spain — long before that region belonged to the nation of Texas, was ceded to the United States in 1850, and was No Man's Land for many years before it became part of Oklahoma Territory in 1890, then finally, in 1907, the Panhandle of Oklahoma.

While the stream has also been called the Red Fork of the Arkansas River, its more established "Cimarron" is reported to be from the Spanish term of *Rio de los Carneros Cimarron,* or "River of the Wild Sheep."

However, it's speculated that, considering how a language changes over some three centuries, the words could have a wider meaning; and if the term did indeed apply to wild animals, could also mean buffalo or mustangs.

The Cimarron, with headwaters in nearby New Mexico, begins where the Dry Cimarron River and Carrizo Creek meet near the western tip of the Panhandle and near Black Mesa, which at 4,973 feet is the state's highest point; and some 12 miles northwest of where the Santa Fe Trail, a traders' route from Missouri into Spanish territory and later a new province of Mexico, crossed the area in about the 1820s.

More than 355 years after the river reportedly got its name, it continued to flow eastward, snaking up into Kansas a few times and meandering across much of northern Oklahoma until joining the Arkansas River and Keystone Lake at Mannford.

Also, "Cimarron," pleasing to many ears, is the name of Edna

Ferber's epic novel about Oklahoma; is the designation of one of the state's turnpikes; and has been the name of at least four state towns.

They include Boise City, which was Cimarron until its name was changed – but the town remained the seat of Cimarron County; and a major event in the Panhandle has been the Cimarron Territory Celebration, held at Beaver, and including the nationally known World Championship Cow Chip Throw.

The name of that celebration refers to an unsuccessful move by settlers in 1887 to organize the Panhandle as "Cimarron Territory." That was three years before the Panhandle became part of Oklahoma Territory, and the entire Panhandle was named Beaver County; and 20 years before Oklahoma statehood, when it encompassed the three counties of Beaver, Texas and Cimarron.

Well into the 21st century, apparently the only state town bearing the river's name was Cimarron City, in Logan County, some 25 miles north of Oklahoma City. It had a population of only about 160, but was on the official state map.

Also, the mayor, Sam Pennington, a retired government employee in his early 70s, indicated local folks were proud of the name. Three of its main streets were Cimarron Boulevard, Cimarron Road and Cimarron Trail.

And a short distance north along the highway was a small business called the Cimarron Bait N' Tackle.

Regarding the origin of the river's name, there's another story – unconfirmed, but lasting:

Once, way out in No Man's Land during a cattle roundup, the cook stopped his chuck wagon and built a fire to prepare a pot of beans, using water from the nearby stream.

But the water wouldn't boil; it just simmered. So all the tired, overworked and frustrated cook could do was stand over the pot and say, "SIMMER ON, beans, SIMMER ON!"

While the story varies, depending on the teller, it's one that has been told countless times, in the Panhandle and "downstate" as well.

But Jack Wiggins, a Panhandle rancher living near Kenton, said he wondered if in modern times it's been told often enough. He considered it a gem of folklore definitely worth handing down.

"I heard that when I was a kid, years ago," said Wiggins, a slow-talking cowman in his late 70s. "You don't hear it much anymore – I guess some of us aren't doing our job by not passin' it along."

Ferdinandina (circa 1719) – A Royal 'Mess'

The site of Ferdinandina is situated some five miles northeast of present-day Newkirk in Kay County in northern Oklahoma, on the west bank of the Arkansas River at the mouth of Deer Creek and at the edge of Kaw Lake; and the name refers to a trading post in what was part of the territory claimed by France during the 18th century. It may have existed as early as 1719.

While it's been called the first white settlement in what is now Oklahoma, many historians say it was a Wichita Indian village, as well as a center for bartering between the Indians and French traders.

It was apparently named for King Ferdinand – or at least one of the long list of Spanish rulers with that royal name.

Nearly 290 years after its reported beginning, the site was better known as the former Traders' Bend Recreation Area – a U.S. Army Corps of Engineers project that, as a park, had been abandoned, leaving the historical area indiscernible in a thicket of trees and brush.

And little local attention was paid to it, and it seemed most of that attention was directed at its physical condition.

And when it was mentioned locally, it often was remembered mostly for its colorful name – and the way it was pronounced, or mispronounced, as well as some of its nicknames.

Karen Dye of Newkirk, a writer of history and curator of both that town's Community Museum and Heritage Center, described the site as that of a Wichita village that had contact with French traders – but not necessarily a French trading post.

"It's perceived as being the first white settlement, but it never was," she said. "However, it makes a fantastic story."

As for its historical significance, Dye said it didn't attract many visitors.

"People used to go there and collect artifacts," she said, "but now the actual site is fenced off, and it's so grown up with weeds you couldn't find anything."

But regardless of what the place was to start with, Harry Wayne Johnston, a local retired farmer and oil company employee in his late 70s, recalled that in more recent times it was a place for wagons and teams and other travelers to cross – if they were careful.

"We just knew there was a crossing there – I was raised a mile down the river," he said. "And lots of people drown there. I helped pull two different guys out of there."

Dye said many people aren't sure about its name.

"It's a long word. 'Fort Fernadina' – that's the way I say it," she said. "And that's what many of the locals call it."

Officials at the Army Corps of Engineers' Kaw Lake office, who acknowledged that the site had been abandoned by the Corps as a park, said they called it "the Deer Creek Site."

It's also been called "Camp Ferdinandina."

Also, over the years the name of the place has also been jokingly likened to "Ferdinand the Bull," the fictional gentle character in the classic storybook for children, "The Story of Ferdinand."

Harry Johnston, though, had still another name for the place: "Fernando Point."

But he agreed with Karen Dye about its condition: "The Corps of Engineers put a fence around it and left it, and it's all grown up in weeds. It's a mess."

San Bernardo (circa 1759) – the Wichitas

San Bernardo, in what eventually became a rural, nondescript area along the Red River in Jefferson County in southern Oklahoma, is believed to have begun in 1778 as an Indian and French settlement when the region was part of Spain.

However, its significant history – particularly to a certain tribe of Indians – begins nearly two decades earlier, with a battle in 1759.

The location of old San Bernardo has long been noted on the official state map as Petersburg, which began as a post office in 1891, and which many years later consisted of a cemetery, a few homes and a small historical monument that described San Bernardo as "Oklahoma's oldest town on Red River."

San Bernardo apparently was named in honor of Bernardo de Galvez, governor of the province of Louisiana after it was ceded to Spain.

However, the place is more significant as the site of what happened in 1759 after Spanish troops attacked an Indian village – a colossal fight won by the Indians.

On a fall day in that year, when the region was still claimed by France, which had settled the Louisiana province, a force of some 600 troops led by Gen. Don Diego Ortiz Parrilla marched northward from deep within New Spain – present-day Texas – and raided the Taovaya Indians.

While the village, on the north bank of the river, was also inhabited by some Frenchmen, the outcome of the battle has long been considered a major victory in the history of Oklahoma's Wichitas, considered descendants of the Taovayas.

The incident has been described by Texas historians as "a victory over Spain," and important because it stopped the northward move of Spanish settlements. Also, various historical reports call it the beginning of the end of Spanish power in the Southern Plains — as well as the peak of Wichita strength.

The Wichitas were to become known as Oklahoma's oldest Indian tribe – and possibly its only native tribe, depending on how the state's history is perceived.

One of two markers near old San Bernardo.

Besides the Wichitas, tribes considered natives of present-day Oklahoma, or who came there on their own, include the Caddos, Comanches, Kiowas and Osages.

These tribes were believed to have some presence in the region before the Indian Removal Act of 1830, and the importation of the so-called Five Civilized Tribes of the Cherokees, Chickasaws, Choctaws, Creeks and Seminoles.

While not all historians agree, that U.S. legislation in 1830, and the westward relocation of an estimated 70,000 Indians from east of the Mississippi River, has not only become synonymous with the term "Trail of Tears" but has been called the establishment of Indian Territory in what finally became Oklahoma.

The forced removal apparently caused many Indian deaths from sickness, starvation and exposure – despite some claims that challenge the "tears" connotation, alleging that such miseries were exaggerated.

Close to 230 years after old San Bernardo's beginning – and nearly 250 years after the battle there — there were still tales of that border region, including many of more recent times.

Kenneth Longest, a resident of the Petersburg area in his mid 60s, recalled stories passed down from his grandfather, Caleb J. Longest, who for a time operated a ferry across the river.

The place was once a popular crossing for Oklahoma residents to bring back liquor from the Texas side – many, when the ferry wasn't operating, fording the river when it was low or at other times floating their wagons and Model T Ford automobiles across.

"There was a lot of people going across – I think that was the closest place down there to cross the river, for whiskey and beer," he said. "And I remember boys a little older than me used to ride horses cross the river."

And Loyd Park, in his early 60s and a resident of Waurika and publisher of *The Ryan Leader* at Ryan, recalled some wilder stories about the region – legends that he called "great and unusual."

"That area of the river is supposed to hold a cavern that goes from one side of the river to the other, and the Indians supposedly buried some of their treasure in it," he said.

"And, I do believe there is a river *beneath* the river that causes the quicksand stories," he added. "And there are some holes of water above that area that, according to some stories, do not have bottoms!"

Navajoe (circa 1760) – The Comanches

Navajoe, once a town at the western edge of the Wichita Mountains and in present-day Jackson County of southwestern Oklahoma, was named for the nearby Navajo Mountain – which legend calls the site of a battle between two Indian tribes, and a story that epitomizes the fighting spirit of the Comanches.

The settlement of Navajoe, a short distance to the west of the mountain, began in about 1886 in what was then part of Texas, and was some two miles across the North Fork of the Red River from the Comanche, Kiowa and Apache lands of Indian Territory.

Both Navajoe — with the "e" added, apparently to avoid confusion with other "Navajo" names – and its namesake of Navajo Mountain have been called some of Oklahoma's most important historical sites.

The battle is believed to have happened there sometime during the middle 1700s, in what was then part of the Louisiana Territory claimed by Spain, when the Comanches defeated a band of Navajos who had invaded from the west.

The Comanches, part of the Shoshone tribe of eastern Wyoming, during the early 1700s had migrated into what was later the Texas Panhandle and the Spanish colony of New Mexico, becoming allies with the Spanish.

Historians say it was perhaps half a century later when the Comanches showed up in what would become Oklahoma, becoming established in present-day western Oklahoma by 1760.

Some years later they were joined in that area by the Kiowas, who also came from the north; and the two tribes, who earlier had been enemies, became allies.

It's been written that the Comanches, after obtaining horses in about 1680, soon came to be called "Lords of the Plains" – and that as horsemen they had "no equal," and were also known as fierce warriors who dominated the Southern Plains.

The history of the Comanches includes a raid in Texas in 1836 when the Indians captured a young girl, Cynthia Ann Parker, who lived for many years with the Comanches, becoming the wife of Chief Peta Nocona, and the mother of Quanah Parker, known as the last great Comanche chief.

Such incidents involving white captives by Indians of present-day Oklahoma, particularly Comanche and Kiowa, have been portrayed in both fact and fiction, inspiring Western novels and epic Hollywood screen versions.

Among them are books by Alan LeMay, including "The Searchers," along with the movie by the same name that is considered a John Wayne classic.

Many years after the Comanches came to the area on their own, as did the Kiowas, they were ordered during the 1867 Medicine Lodge Treaty to a reservation in the same region – the Comanche, Kiowa and Apache lands, in what then had become Indian Territory.

Regarding the battle linked with the name Navajo Mountain, it's been said the Comanches caught the Navajos trying to steal their horses, and quickly killed or ran off the raiders – except for one, according to a local legend.

A story that's been told for many years is that one Navajo warrior hid atop the mountain – where his ghost would always remain.

Yale Spottedbird Jr., a Kiowa of Hobart, once had discussed the basis for the legend: "All them Navajos was wiped out, but this one."

When the settlement of Navajoe began, among its first stores in 1886 was one operated by two brothers-in-law, W.H. Acre and H.P. Dale – whose younger brother, Edward Everett Dale, became a noted author and Oklahoma historian. Navajoe's post office opened on Sept. 1, 1887.

It was then officially part of Texas, but had ties to the nearby territory that would someday be called Oklahoma.

Helping to settle Navajoe was colorful land promoter Joseph S. "Buckskin Joe" Works, who lured emigrants to what he called the "Texas-Oklahoma Colony."

The area it occupied, which was south and west of the North Fork of the Red, was then the previously described Greer County, Texas, which some years later would become Indian Territory, then Oklahoma Territory and finally Oklahoma.

For a while Navajoe was known as a typical wild Texas town, with its occasional gunfights and other rowdy goings on, plus regular horse races between the Comanche and Kiowa Indians and the white settlers. The Indians would come in and pitch their tepees outside of town, and a track that surrounded the town was soon well worn.

More than 245 years after the conjectured date of the Navajo Mountain battle, the town of Navajoe was gone (the post office had

Monument at Navajoe.

closed in 1905), but it was still on the official state map – but this time spelled without the "e."

And the region boasted a nice, 12-grade Navajoe school system, a cemetery with a large gate, and a historical marker just as impressive, a few homes and several acres of pasture and farmland.

Sam C. Howard, a longtime local resident and farmer in his early 90s, seemed to be the best local historian. His grandfather, A.L. Howard, one of the early settlers there, was shot in the back and killed in 1890 by an itinerant gambler in front of the local saloon.

However, Sam also knew a lot about the battle between the Indians – as did many history enthusiasts in that part of the state.

Sue Jones of nearby Altus, a writer and veteran historian, called Navajo Mountain an important, but overlooked chapter in Oklahoma history.

"To me it's fascinating that more hasn't been done about it, like in movies and stuff," she said.

Sam Howard called the story especially interesting because the Navajos invaded the local Indians' territory – "but got whupped themselves."

He added: "Those Comanches were pretty tough guys."

Rainy Mountain (circa 1797) – The Kiowas

Rainy Mountain, near present-day Mountain View in Kiowa County, is the name of a quiet area in the southwestern part of the state that has been called the home of the Kiowa people of Oklahoma.

Some tribal historians believe the region surrounding a bare hill was named in the late 1790s by the Kiowas when they settled there, in what was then part of Spain's Louisiana Territory – long before that region would become the Comanche, Kiowa and Apache reservation of Indian Territory, and later of Oklahoma Territory.

According to legend, this tribe of Indians had migrated from their original home in the far north – possibly the Yellowstone River country of central Montana, or maybe even Canada – via the Black Hills.

Rainy Mountain also symbolizes a major change in the ways of the Kiowa. As former mountain people, when they came there they adapted to life on the plains.

Also, it's believed that it was during their trek from the north that they abandoned traveling with dogs and travoises and obtained horses – and the Kiowas, like the Comanches, became as noted for their horsemanship as for their fighting.

One story about how Rainy Mountain was named has it that the first Kiowas to approach the area were some warriors on their way to Texas on a war journey.

According to Ernestine Kauahquo Kauley of Hobart, a tribal historian and great-granddaughter of Kiowa Chief Lone Wolf (Kooie-pah-gaw), the hill was where the war party "stopped to fast and pray – and it rained and rained and rained."

Nearly 210 years after the supposed naming of Rainy Mountain, the area was comprised of a cemetery, the Rainy Mountain Kiowa Indian Baptist Church and the old foundation of the Rainy Mountain

School, which the U.S. government had established in 1893, when missionaries came to present-day southwestern Oklahoma.

Buried at Rainy Mountain were such noted Kiowas as Big Tree (Ah-daw-ate), a well-known chief; Jack Bointy (Boyen-tday), another tribal leader; and Cornelius Spottedhorse (Tsain-pope-tday), tribal song leader.

The Kiowas, like the Comanches, often took captives during battles, and other names on tombstones at Rainy Mountain included those of such captives as Sain-toh-oodle (English name Millie Durgan); and To-goam-gatty (Mary Hamleton). Taken as children, both had married into the tribe and spent their remaining lives as Kiowas.

Sain-toh-oodle, meaning "Killed with Blunt Arrow," and later referred to as "Mrs. Goombi," was seized as a baby during an Indian raid on a settlers' cabin in North Texas in 1864.

To-goam-gatty (misspelled "Tagonegatty" on her tombstone), meaning "Woman Who Stands Behind Tepee," also was taken as a young girl in a raid on a white family in Texas, in 1867.

Buried next to her was her husband, Calisay, another captive, and who was believed taken during a raid in Mexico (his non-Indian name may have been Carlos).

Some 140 years after the captures of Millie Durgan and Mary Hamleton, both had descendants in southwestern Oklahoma, including two men in their 60s who were prominent tribal members.

Sain-toh-oodle's great-grandson, J.T. Goombi of Anadarko, was a teacher of Kiowa culture who had served as tribal chairman in the late 1980s and early '90s.

George Tahbone of Mountain View, a grandson of To-goam-gatty, was a former member of the Kiowa Business Committee and had been known as an Indian dancer in both Oklahoma and Texas.

For many reasons, the general area of the cemetery and church is special within the tribe, according to Atwater Onco of Elgin, a respected Kiowa elder in his early 80s who was writing a history of Rainy Mountain.

Regardless of exactly when, or how Rainy Mountain was named, to Kiowas it's where, during the spring, summer and fall, breezes stir the cedar and mesquite trees and whisper of the past – a place of dreams, and prayers.

Renowned author N. Scott Momaday, the part Kiowa native of

southwestern Oklahoma who later lived in Tucson, Arizona, had written in his book, "The Way to Rainy Mountain":

"A single knoll rises out of the plain of Oklahoma. For my people, the Kiowas, it is an old landmark. To look upon that landscape in the early morning, with the sun at your back, is to lose the sense of proportion. Your imagination comes to life, and this, you think, is where Creation was begun."

Sequoyah (circa 1829) – The Cherokees

Sequoyah can be thought of as a place that existed in the eastern part of Indian Territory, but is more meaningful as the name of a man – one who could be considered the ultimate symbol of the Cherokees, the largest Indian tribe in Oklahoma and among the most progressive of the Five Civilized Tribes.

As the inventor of the Cherokee alphabet – or "Talking Leaves" — Sequoyah, a half-blood Cherokee, has been honored with portrayals in the Oklahoma State Capitol as well as the nation's Capitol in Washington, D.C.

When he came to present-day Oklahoma, in about 1829, he brought along his newly compiled list of characters — or letters — that put the sounds of the Cherokee language into writing.

Sequoyah, also known as George Guess and whose Cherokee name is said to mean "shut in or away," came from someplace in the Appalachians. It's believed that he first migrated to present-day Arkansas, and that he and several other Cherokees then moved farther west to what would soon be called Indian Territory.

He apparently was among the members of his tribe who came early – becoming known as the Western Cherokees – as opposed to an estimated 16,000 tribal members who were moved by the U.S. government to Indian Territory in 1838 and 1839, and were called the Eastern Cherokees.

In September of 1839, the Eastern and Western Cherokees met at Tahlequah to sign a new constitution, and Tahlequah became the permanent capital of the Cherokee Nation.

His former home in present-day Oklahoma is a refurbished log cabin that is a historical site near Sallisaw – the seat of the county named for him. It's on the official state map as Home of Sequoyah, plus is also called Sequoyah's Cabin.

In addition, Sequoyah was once the name signifying the center of a district of the Cherokee Nation. It was near Muldrow, and close to Skin Bayou, a tributary of the Arkansas River.

Also, Sequoyah nearly became the name of a state. In 1905, leaders of the Five Civilized Tribes – often referred to as the "Indian Nations" – officially proposed statehood for that region of Indian Territory.

The name Sequoyah has indeed been revered among the Cherokee people. Among those who have been named in his honor is Sequoyah Houston (the last name another word dear to many Cherokees), a well-known tribal lawman who was killed in a shoot-out with the notorious "Cook gang" of outlaws in 1894.

More than 175 years after the supposed establishment of Sequoyah's home in Indian Territory, that part of Oklahoma included the Home of Sequoyah, the Oklahoma Historical Society's site on State Highway 101 about 10 miles northeast of Sallisaw.

It was visited by an estimated 20,000 people a year, "from all around the world," said curator Jerry Dobbs.

And, a short distance to the northwest in neighboring Cherokee County was the heart of the Cherokee Nation of Oklahoma. It included the old Cherokee National Capitol building in Tahlequah – and not far away, the several facilities of the newer tribal headquarters.

That overall complex, described in a smart Web site, was the epitome of 21st century sophistication. It included the headquarters of Principal Chief Chad Smith and other business offices near Tahlequah; plus the Cherokee Heritage Center at nearby Park Hill, with such attractions as a museum, the Tsa-La-Gi Ancient Village, and an outdoor theater for presentation of an annual "Trail of Tears" Drama.

The 52nd annual Cherokee National Holiday was being planned, which would include a public history conference sponsored partly by the Great State of Sequoyah Commission, the commission members including past chief Wilma Mankiller.

It was one of many ways the Cherokees saluted their heritage, including the man called Sequoyah.

Wigwam Neosho (circa 1829) – Sam Houston

Wigwam Neosho was a trading post that once was somewhere in present-day Wagoner County of eastern Oklahoma, and which was operated by Sam Houston shortly before he went south to become one of the most famous names in the history of Texas.

The trading post is believed to have first existed in 1829, in what was then land that the United States had ceded to the Choctaws, a year before it became known as Indian Territory. The trading post apparently operated for about four years.

It was situated a short distance north of what for many years was called the Three Forks region, rear the confluence of the Neosho, Arkansas and Verdigris rivers, and was named for the Neosho, an Osage word meaning "clear water."

The Neosho, which is believed to have earlier been known as "Six Bulls," was to finally become known as the Grand River.

Neosho was also the name of a district of the Cherokee Nation that was established before 1831, and, like the trading post, took its name from the river.

Wigwam Neosho is the place where Houston, a former governor of Tennessee and a friend of the Cherokees, lived and took a Cherokee wife, Tiana Rogers, in about 1830, some two years before he left and became a Texas hero.

He helped to win that region's independence from Mexico, and was to be named the first president of the Republic of Texas – and 23 years later, to become governor of the state of Texas.

It's believed that the trading post was also visited by noted writer Washington Irving, who during 1832 was doing research for his "A Tour on the Prairies."

More than 175 years after the reported beginning of Wigwam Neosho, a state historical marker that told of the place stood along U.S. Highway 69 a mile north of the Arkansas River – but it seemed history enthusiasts would never agree on where the old trading post had been.

Some local historians believed the site of Wigwam Neosho, while difficult to determine, was atop one of several rises between the towns of Okay and Fort Gibson.

Gary Moore, a part-time interpreter for the Oklahoma Historical Society's site at Fort Gibson, suggested the old trading post was on "a high slope that has never been plowed, on grazing land, or hay land, you might say."

Not that there were many historians to argue about it. Wigwam Neosho, it seemed, had virtually been forgotten.

Wally Waits, a specialist in local history at the Muskogee Public Library, said that over a period of nearly 15 years, "I've only heard two or three people say they knew a thing about Neosho."

Gene Coffey of near Okay, a retired military man in his early 70s, agreed. He said he and his wife, Nancy, who belonged to the Three Forks Treasure Hunters' Club, believed they had found the location of the old trading post – and there was no one to argue with them.

"You don't hear many people mention it anymore," he said. And he added that the few who did, would say things like "Why was it called 'wigwam'?"

Eagle Town (circa 1832) – The Choctaws

Eagle Town was settled in the early 1830s in the Choctaw Nation of Indian Territory, its post office being established on July 1, 1834.

Over the years the spelling of the post office and town changed to Eagletown, and its location would finally be in McCurtain County of southeastern Oklahoma.

It's believed it was so named because many eagles nested there – either in the trees along the nearby Mountain Fork River, or virtually right in town, in a very large tree.

But Eagle Town's historical importance is that it is where the Choctaws, during their relocation from the area of Mississippi, entered Indian Territory during the early 1830s.

It's also significant as the site of Stockbridge Mission, established in 1836, where missionary and Choctaw linguist Cyrus Byington composed his "Choctaw Definer," an English-Choctaw dictionary that was published in 1852.

It was also where Jefferson Gardner, who was principal chief of the Choctaws in the mid 1890s, lived and operated a store.

Close to 175 years after its beginning, Eagletown was a village of the post office and a few convenience stores, along with the historic Gardner Mansion, plus the trunk of a huge cypress that at one time had been called the state's largest tree – about 150 feet tall and 43 feet around at the base – and, with an estimated age of 2,000 years, possibly the oldest tree.

The area also had at least one resident with a big interest in local history – Dr. Lewis Stiles, a veterinarian in his middle 70s who also was a past president of the Oklahoma Historical Society.

He also was owner and curator of the Gardner Mansion, which included a museum inside; and he lived within about 50 feet of the edge of what once was part of Eagle Town.

Stiles said he regularly told the many visitors to the site such things as Eagletown having "the oldest post office in Oklahoma that's still in operation."

He also said visitors often would ask him about the name of the place, and that his answer was "that eagles nested in this big tree when the first Choctaws came here – at least, that's the legend."

And that could be true, as he said he still saw eagles there occasionally – in some seasons and under certain conditions, "four to six of them every morning."

Cutthroat Gap (1833) – A Sad 'Presence'

Cutthroat Gap, in a valley in present-day southwestern Oklahoma with a beauty and calm that have been called ghostly, is both the name of a place and a chilling description of an 1833 slaughter of about 150 human beings.

In the spring of that year, in what was then the southwestern portion of Indian Territory, a Kiowa village – while occupied mostly by old people and children – was annihilated in a surprise and bloody attack by an Osage raiding party. The defenseless Kiowas were slain, and beheaded.

The warriors of the village, who were away on a warring venture of their own when the attack occurred, returned to find the camp burned and their family members mutilated – and their heads in brass buckets.

More than 170 years later, a granite stone memorial had been placed along State Highway 54 a short distance south of Cooperton. It told of the massacre and the site, east of there along Otter Creek at the edge of the Wichita Mountains, in northwestern Comanche County.

But the monument, erected in the late 1990s, wasn't necessary as a reminder, observers said.

"It's the worst tragedy in the history of the Kiowas," said Jack Haley, a rancher of Roosevelt and owner of the site. Haley, in his early 70s, also had been president of the Oklahoma Historical Society.

"There's not a Kiowa living today that doesn't have a family member or relative that was in that," he said. "Most of them have an ancestor that was a victim."

Many Kiowas, however, believed such a memorial was appropriate, and the monument was sponsored by tribal members Doris Poolaw and Dorothy Whitehorse Delvan, with participation by Haley.

For several years, Kiowa people had considered the site of the massacre sacred and had come to pay their respect, where their ancestors are buried in a mass grave, said Haley, who allowed them to visit the region.

"They are fewer and fewer, but about once or twice a year the older Kiowas would never miss visiting the area, especially after dark," he said – explaining that after dark was believed to be the time when "the spirits are still roaming – though with their heads off, and incomplete."

"And for years and years," he said, "one man would come, and go to the top of one of the mountains before sundown – and sing and pray till sunrise."

Haley said he visited the area often as well, and that he believed it has changed little since the tragic event occurred; it was at a time when the weather was warming and the wild plums were ripening.

Haley, who called himself part Indian – Cherokee – said he understood such feelings about the site of the tragedy.

"I don't make light of these things," he said. "I think there's a presence there at times."

Boggy Depot (circa 1837) – 'On the Boggy'

Boggy Depot apparently was first settled in 1837 by Cyrus Harris, who later would become governor of the Chickasaw Nation, when he built his log cabin home there in what was then the Choctaw Nation of Indian Territory.

A post office was established there on Nov. 5, 1849, and some 58 years later the area would be described as in Atoka County of southeastern Oklahoma.

Boggy Depot apparently was named for nearby Clear Boggy Creek, believed to be named from a French word meaning "muddy" — and the names strike some observers as contradictory.

And over the years residents of that area have been familiar with similar, related terms such as Big Boggy, Little Boggy, Middle Boggy and Muddy Boggy.

For many years (until 1872 when it was bypassed by a railroad) what was often called "the Depot on the Boggy" was one of the most important settlements in Indian Territory. It was the government's depot for handling annuities and supplies, plus was on the routes of both the Butterfield Overland Stage Line and the Texas Road.

Also, during the Civil War, the Confederates used it as a military post and major commissary depot.

It also served as the temporary capital of the Choctaw Nation, plus for a time it was the home of Rev. Allen Wright (Kiliahote), who would become known as the distinguished chief of the Choctaws and the creator of the name of the future state of Oklahoma.

Boggy Depot was the namesake of a Civil War battle fought in the general area – the Battle of Middle Boggy.

After the war, historians say, the first Masonic Lodge in present-day Oklahoma was organized there, in 1872.

Nearly 170 years after Boggy Depot was said to be named, the place was represented by the Boggy Depot State Park, about 15 miles southwest of Atoka – as well as the "Boggy" streams in that area, along with observations.

Ronnie Anderson, a resident of Caney, said he had heard older relatives "talk about Boggy – Muddy and Clear both – where they went catfishin' a lot."

Anderson, an Army retiree in his early 60s, also told of a personal experience on Clear Boggy.

At times, he said, "it *is* clear –but you get down the bank, and I'll guarantee you, it's boggy!"

Going Snake (circa 1839) – A Memorable Name

Going Snake was at first the name of a district of the Cherokee Nation of Indian Territory, believed to have been created by the Cherokee National Council in the late 1830s, the district covering virtually all of Adair County and part of Cherokee County in what now is eastern Oklahoma.

It was named for Going Snake, (In-na-tah-oolo-sah) a prominent chief of the Eastern Cherokees who also was once speaker of the Cherokee Council.

His name – but spelled as one word – many years later also designated a small community near present-day Westville in Adair County, and named for the Going Snake district. The Goingsnake post office was established on May 5, 1890, in what was then the Cherokee Nation of Indian Territory.

Going Snake, who has been described as "one of the oldest and most beloved chiefs to make the Trail of Tears journey of 1838," is among the famous names in the history and culture of the Cherokees.

Various organizations and establishments bear the name, such as the Goingsnake Historical Society, Goingsnake Historical District Association, Goingsnake District Heritage Association, and its publication, *The Goingsnake Messenger*. It's also been the name of a school, and there's a Goingsnake Creek.

The written history involving the name Going Snake is extensive. It includes interpretations on such reported incidents as "the Tragedy of the Goingsnake District," also known as "the Goingsnake Massacre."

Those terms refer to the 1872 murder trial of Ezekiel "Zeke" Proctor, which turned into a wild melee and shoot-out when several of his enemies, known as the "Beck faction," stormed the Whitmire Schoolhouse where the session was being held.

According to various reports, between nine and 12 persons were killed, with victims on both sides, and several wounded, including Proctor.

The trial continued the following day, and Proctor, a former Cherokee Nation sheriff accused in the accidental killing of a woman, was acquitted.

"Going Snake" also has inspired books, among them "The Witch of Goingsnake and Other Stories," by Robert J. Conley of Tahlequah.

More than 165 years after Going Snake became an established name in present-day Oklahoma, there was virtually no sign of the Goingsnake town that began in 1890, its post office having closed four years later. The site was a few miles west of Westville in an area called Strawberry Springs.

But at Westville itself was the grave of Chief Going Snake.

"And we just recently commemorated that," said Glenita Guthrie of Westville, editor of *The Goingsnake Messenger,* noting that officials of both the heritage association and the Cherokee Trail of Tears Association took part in the special ceremonies.

She agreed that the name Goingsnake – whether spelled one word or two – isn't likely to be forgotten in her part of the state.

Antelope Hills (circa 1849) — Animals, Art and Stories

The Antelope Hills, a family of rugged mounds that juts from the prairie of western Oklahoma, apparently have been called that since 1849.

Some historians say that probably would have been when gold hunters, mainly from the Southern states, had begun to head westward on the California Road, crossing what was then a portion of Indian Territory that was meant for the Seminoles, but occupied by the Kiowas and other Plains tribes.

The hills, covering about 10 square miles of rangeland in a bend of the Canadian River that separates Roger Mills and Ellis counties, and near portions of the Black Kettle National Grassland, have long been a local landmark and an attraction for tourists, as well as historians.

Written history says at one time the hills were known as the "Boundary Mountains," being along the international border between the United States and Mexico; and then in 1847, during some of the first rushes to California, they were called "Pilot Hills."

After what possibly was the first time the Antelope Hills were called that in 1849, it's believed the name was well known in 1858 when Texas Rangers routed a band of Comanche warriors in the hills; in 1868 when Army Lt. Col. George A. Custer and his cavalry troops passed the area to ravage the snow-covered village of Chief Black Kettle and his Southern Cheyennes on an early November morning in what history would later call the Battle of the Washita; and in 1874 when Army soldiers fought Indians in the same region.

Also, according to early-day brand registrations, cattlemen referred to the Antelope Hills when they came to the area nearly 20 years later, when the Cheyenne and Arapaho lands of Oklahoma Territory were opened to settlement by a land run on April 19, 1892.

The hills have been on the state's official highway map since 1932 — and in recent years, placed on the National Register of Historic

Places, through the efforts of Melvena Thurman Heisch, deputy state historic preservation officer with the Oklahoma Historical Society.

As geographic features normally don't receive such recognition, the hills weren't immediately accepted on the list – but finally were when Heisch, who is a native of nearby Reydon, insisted they were "important, as a landmark through time."

While it's believed antelopes were in the vicinity of the hills in years past, in 1996 the state's Department of Wildlife Conservation began replenishing the "appropriately named" Antelope Hills with the fleet-footed animals by making a trade – some Rio Grande turkeys from Oklahoma for some pronghorn antelope from Wyoming.

More than 155 years after the Antelope Hills were apparently given that name, the hills remained a beacon in a quiet, thinly populated area – but were near a $250,000 art gallery and museum that had opened not many years earlier.

The Break O'Day Farm and Metcalfe Museum was dedicated to the memory of Augusta Corson Metcalfe, who, while making a living in a rough land, depicted pioneer life in a rugged land with sketches and paintings and became famous as "the sagebrush artist."

She was featured in *LIFE* magazine in 1950, and was inducted into the Oklahoma Hall of Fame as well as the National Cowgirl Hall of Fame.

Among the displays of her artwork is at least one picture of the Antelope Hills, said Elaine Adams of Durham, founder and past board president of the museum.

And the hills continued to attract sightseers and people who in general fancied beauty in nature.

Jack Sorenson, a nationally known Western artist of Amarillo,

Texas, recalled when he visited the Antelope Hills some 30 years earlier, while taking lessons from Dord Fitz, a retired art teacher from the University of Kentucky who lived in the hills.

And local residents still swapped opinions, memories and stories about the hills.

Max Montgomery, a Durham rancher in his late 50s, and whose wife, Janna, was the Metcalfe museum's board president, had a map showing the Antelope Hills in 1849.

However, Max said he believed Comancheros, and not gold seekers, "came up with the name of Antelope Hills – and I'm sure there were plenty of antelopes there at that time."

June Hartley, who with husband Charlie lived on a ranch in the hills, said the antelopes – whether from the Wyoming imports or native animals – were still there, along with other creatures, such as "deer, turkey, armadillos and owls, and coyotes, too."

Jo Nell York said she and her husband, Donnie, had ranched in that area for many years, and still found the hills interesting, as well as "stories about gold buried here – but I don't know about that."

Calvin Bachmann, a native of the Durham area in his middle 60s who ran the Hitchin' Post store, said his grandfather, George Gantz, had talked of buried treasure.

"Grandpaw talked about gold, and he believed it," Bachmann said. "I think he knew the guys who were digging for it. But I just remember enough to be confused about it."

Gordon Thomas, a Reydon rancher in his middle 50s, recalled playing in the hills as a boy, but said he had become more interested in the stories about gold.

Ike Lucas, a retired Durham area rancher in the middle 70s, told a "chili con carne" story about the Antelope Hills:

The early-day Spanish explorer Coronado came through, "and he ran out of grub, so he sent Poncho, his head cook, out to look. Poncho found a dead buffalo – it'd been dead for a while – and he had a load of chili peppers on his burro, so he made a whole batch of that, with the old meat and the chili. And Coronado thought it was good!"

Lucas added: "I've told that lie so many times I almost believe it myself."

Packsaddle Crossing (circa 1858) – A Span of Theories

Packsaddle Crossing – at first simply called a crossing, and later the name of a bridge, a wildlife preserve and even a community of sorts – is located in western Oklahoma on the Canadian River where U.S. Highway 283 crosses the stream where it separates the counties of Ellis and Roger Mills.

Its name may go back to the aforementioned 1858 fight between the Texas Rangers and Comanches in that part of Indian Territory. It's been said that the Rangers, while near either the river or a nearby creek, found a packsaddle that had been taken during an Indian raid on a Texas ranch.

Old-timers who held with that theory included the late John Dunn, who had heard of such an incident when he came through present-day western Oklahoma as a Texas cowhand on the Great Western Trail. The story, which also mentioned a "Packsaddle Creek," was passed on by his son, the late John Dunn Jr., a Woodward rancher.

However, another belief is that the crossing was named by Custer during his previously described 1868 campaign to wipe out the Cheyenne village, when he and his soldiers found a packsaddle – or possibly several of them – at the river on their way either to or from the battle site.

Still another theory is that early-day freighters, in order to cross the river when it was dangerously high, would unload their wagons and put the goods on pack animals, for swimming the loads across. The freighters would either float the empty wagons to the other bank or leave them behind.

In 1930, Packsaddle Bridge was built and dedicated at the site. Nearly a mile long, it was considered the longest of its type in Oklahoma.

In 1985, the old bridge, after being partially destroyed by a large tank truck, was replaced by a new span that was christened the Bradshaw-Packsaddle Bridge, named for the late State Rep. Mark "Buzz" Bradshaw of Arnett.

About five years later, the Packsaddle Wildlife Management Area was established by the state on the north side of the river.

For a time over the years, the region was also the site of a small business, the Packsaddle Bar.

Close to 150 years after its possible naming, the old Packsaddle Crossing was mainly comprised of the 1985 bridge that formed an im-

posing arc above the river, and the wildlife management area. The overall region was thinly populated and usually quiet.

Scott Parry, a wildlife biologist in his middle 30s who was manager of the wildlife management area, said he had heard some of the theories behind the Packsaddle name, and that "I'd say any one of them could be believable — but then they can't all be true."

Rich Patterson, a cowman and horse trainer in his middle 60s whose home was nearby, spoke of recorded local history and numerous animal bones and mule shoes discovered in a canyon.

He didn't claim to know the exact origin of the name, but said he felt sure "there's gotta be something to all that business."

Patterson, and a few others who lived just north of the river, were considered residents of a place with a definite identity.

When asked their address, they often were fond of saying "I'm from Packsaddle!"

Tamaha (1864) – The Steamboat

Tamaha, in present-day Haskell County of eastern Oklahoma, was once a settlement along the Arkansas River in the Choctaw Nation of Indian Territory, and is significant because it's a Choctaw word for "town."

However, it's better known as the place where Confederate troops captured a Union steamboat during the Civil War.

Reports have it that Indian troops representing the Confederates, who were on a high bank above the river, attacked the *J.R. Williams*, an armed Union boat, on June 15, 1864. The Southern troops, with cannons and possibly other firepower, rendered the boat defenseless, and the craft apparently sank to the bottom.

The town of Tamaha didn't exist at that time, but it's believed a boat landing of sorts was there for several years, and the attack on the steamboat has been called the beginning of the community's history – although it was two decades later that Tamaha officially began. Its post office opened on April 17, 1884.

Besides the Civil War incident, Tamaha's history includes the report of an early-day bank robbery, of two fires over the years that nearly razed the whole town, and a story about the old town jail that's been told over and over.

It was said the jail's first prisoner was the local mail carrier, Frank Prentice, after he became too intoxicated to deliver the mail – galloping into town on horseback, with all the letters fluttering out of his open saddlebags.

He was jailed, as the new jail's first prisoner, and the small rock building was named after him: "Fort Prentice."

More than 140 years after the steamboat incident at the site of Tamaha, it was a tiny place with a calming ambiance on the bank of what had become the McClellan-Kerr Arkansas River Navigation System. It was a favorite spot for many fishermen and pleasure boaters.

Tamaha's post office had closed in 1954, but it was still on the official state map. The community was comprised of a store, a few churches, a senior citizens center and volunteer fire department, which often had been supported by an annual fish fry.

And the historical attraction in town was the small rock building with the established nickname of Fort Prentice.

However, probably most local talk was about the steamboat, according to Nan Stone at the Bonnie & Clyde Tamaha General Store. She ran the place with the help of her mother and sister, Diane Bishop and Debbie Hudspeth, respectfully.

"Depending on who you talk to," Nan said, "the smoke stack of that boat can still be seen when the water's low."

But there was a story of her own that she took more seriously – about a cannonball on display in her store.

She said a fisherman found it, and it was determined to be Confederate ammunition – "so we say 'This is the one that sank the *J.R. Williams.*'"

"And who," she added, "can prove that it isn't?"

Camp Napoleon (1865) – Big Powwow

Camp Napoleon was the location of a large peace conference between two groups of Indians in May 1865, and the site eventually became Verden, in Grady County in Oklahoma's southwestern quadrant.

Camp Napoleon is remembered both for its uncommon name and because it represents a major event in the history of Oklahoma and its Indians.

It reportedly was named for Mexican Emperor Maximilian, a puppet of Napoleon III, supposedly because an envoy of the emperor attended the meeting.

While history isn't clear about the eventual outcome of the conference, it was aimed at achieving peace between the Indian Territory people and the Plains tribes – and particularly to halt fighting triggered by divided loyalties during the Civil War. It was said that a slogan voiced during the gathering was "An Indian shall not spill an Indian's blood."

The location of the conference was at the eastern edge of what was then designated as the Leased District of Indian Territory, which was Choctaw land leased to the United States as a future home for Wichitas and possibly other tribes.

The Camp Napoleon site also was reported for a time to be a place where white settlers and Indians frequently would meet to exchange captives.

The site became Verden in 1899, when the region had become the Comanche, Kiowa and Apache lands of Oklahoma Territory. Its post office opened on May 5 of that year.

More than 140 years after the Camp Napoleon camp was established, Verden was a small town where residents were more impressed by recent history than by talk of old Camp Napoleon, according to municipal clerk Dian Winkler – although she noted an impressive monument still marked the site of the 1865 peace conference.

Viola Blevins, a local resident in her early 90s, pointed out how the community had become less active since the days when she was a teen-ager.

"This whole country was in cotton," she said. "And there were lots of people in Verden on Saturday – you couldn't hardly get down the street."

Robbers' Roost (1867) – 'Blast 'em Out!'

Robbers' Roost is the name of a fortified nest of outlaws that once existed along Carrizo Creek at the edge of Black Mesa in the western end of No Man's Land.

The spot, near the present-day tiny community of Kenton in Cimarron County of the Oklahoma Panhandle, is where an Army cannon was used in 1867 to crush the rocky hideout of the renegades and end their reign of terror.

Robbers' Roost – possibly given that name by either civilian or military authorities – was a large, customized cave that for some three years had been the seemingly invincible home and headquarters of the Bill Coe outlaw gang.

It's believed that Coe, whose first name has been reported as both William and Cyrus, was the leader because he was the brightest and most daring of the group of criminals. He was often referred to as "Captain Bill Coe."

The mob of bandits, which at one time may have numbered up to 50 members, plagued wagon trains on the Santa Fe Trail, homesteaders, cattlemen and sheepmen, and even military posts in the two neighboring territories of New Mexico and Colorado.

The hideout, at what was called Lookout Peak, or Lookout Point, had been modified with additional, thick walls, with holes to fit rifles, for shooting at invaders – and designed for lavish comfort as well.

It's believed the place even included two grand fireplaces, a large room with a bar and piano. It's said that at times women from Mexico were brought in for dancing and other entertainment.

The Robbers' Roost bunch possibly was at its peak during or after 1865, about the time of the closing of nearby Fort Nichols, whose mission had been to protect travelers on the Santa Fe Trail, from both outlaws and Indians.

The gang apparently began to lose out against law and order sometime after their brazen acts of stealing horses and mules from Fort Union and Fort Lyon in the territories of New Mexico and Colorado, respectfully.

Historians say authorities – either lawmen or soldiers – caught 11 of the bandits one day when they were sleeping in an abandoned adobe hut, and summarily hanged them to the nearest trees they could find.

But the climax of the fall of Robbers' Roost occurred early one morning in late 1867, when an Army detachment from Fort Lyon rolled a six-inch cannon up the mesa for a good shot, and fired — turning the hideout into a heap of dust and rubble.

That, in effect, was the end of the gang, except for Coe, who escaped – but wouldn't enjoy his freedom for long.

He was captured the next year, either in Madison (later Folsum, New Mexico), or in Colorado Territory, where he was held for a short while at Pueblo.

It was at Pueblo, historians say, that he was taken from jail and lynched to a cottonwood tree.

Nearly 140 years after the Robbers' Roost era ended with a cannon blast, only part of its foundation was visible, but the incident remained one of the historical attractions in the Panhandle that visitors find interesting.

"It's probably more popular than the Black Mesa itself – most of the people ask about it," said Allan Griggs, operator of the Kenton Mercantile store.

Griggs, a 60-year-old area resident who also was owner of the land where the old hideout was situated, said the site, along with nearby old Fort Nichols, was an attraction during guided tours of that part of the Panhandle.

Monty Joe Roberts, a longtime area resident, said Robbers' Roost was simply an ideal hideout for a gathering of no-account human beings.

"Like my dad (William M., nicknamed "Monty") used to say, they were just a bunch of drunks and gamblers that would rob travelers and settlers, and then lay up here and drink," said Roberts, a rancher in his late 60s who with wife Vicki also ran the Black Mesa Bed and Breakfast.

Also, he said, "this was a pretty good place to hide out, with nothing out here. Nobody could sneak up on 'em — that was the main thing."

Ghost Mound (circa 1867) – The Rise of Legends

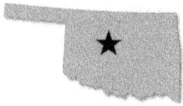

Ghost Mound is a distinctive peak of hard red earth that's known for creepy legends.

It's situated in present-day Caddo County not very far west of the center of Oklahoma, and it may have been named in the late 1860s when it was part of the Wichita and Caddo lands of Indian Territory.

That's about when, according to a compilation of local stories, some tragic deaths happened there, to result in everlasting eerie sounds and sights.

One legend is that a wagon train was attacked by Indians in the area and that a woman and her child were killed, and their screams continue to be heard.

Another is that two Indian brothers were camped near the mound when their horses strayed, and one went after them, but somehow was killed – and returned late at night in the form of a visible spirit.

Still another story is that a young Indian maiden, while she and her lover were watching the sunset from the top of the mound, slipped and fell 285 feet to her death. It's said that the print of her foot – made in her final step – is embedded in the very top of the rise.

It's suspected that some of the mound's ghostlike sightings are of this world – as owls have been spotted flying out of small caves, their white bellies flashing in the darkness.

But, say believers in at least one of the legends, the owls don't erase the print of a moccasin.

Nearly 140 years after the supposed naming of Ghost Mound, it remained a prominent land feature in the prairie country south of Hydro and within sight of State Highway 58.

Deon Yearwood, a farmer in his middle 50s who owned the property, said he still got occasional questions from visitors to his place.

"I don't try to explain the name of Ghost Mound; I just tell about the legends that were told to me," he said – adding, however, that he could still see what resembled the footprint in the stone.

Also, he said the owls that occasionally occupied the mound had been joined by buzzards.

On warm days, the large vultures perched on top, spreading their wings to catch the breeze – a picture, observers said, that further enhanced the picturesque spookiness of Ghost Mound.

Left Hand Spring (1868) – The Chisholm Trail

Left Hand Spring, in what was once a spot along the North Fork of the Canadian River in the Cheyenne and Arapaho lands of Indian Territory, is said to be where Jesse Chisholm died on April 4, 1868, and was buried.

Chisholm, part Scotch and part Cherokee, was visiting the camp of his Arapaho Indian friend, Chief Left Hand, and apparently became fatally ill after eating bear grease that was contaminated by a brass pot. Chisholm's age at death was approximately 63.

Left Hand Spring, along with what's left of the modest gravestone of Jesse Chisholm, symbolizes his namesake, the great Chisholm Trail, the onetime path for millions of Texas long-horned cattle being driven to Kansas – and the name that became world famous and the heart of countless portrayals of the Old West, in song, on the pages of books and on the silver screen.

The historical site, off U.S. Highway 281 and near present-day Greenfield, in Blaine County, is at the base of a sandy rise overlooking the river (now called the North Canadian), a little west of the center of Oklahoma.

While the exact location of his remains, along with the date of his death (some reports say he died in March), has been debated, many historians believe his gravestone is close enough to his final resting place.

The site is near where Chisholm apparently mined salt, and is approximately 40 miles west of where he had a cabin and trading post, at Council Grove (the present-day western portion of Oklahoma City) – and some 15 miles west of the former trail itself, which roughly is paralleled by today's U.S. Highway 81.

Chisholm, a freighter with a chain of several wagons, had partially followed an earlier path of Wichita Indians – becoming known in history as the Wichita Trace – and the later path of Black Beaver, a Delaware Indian who was a scout for the U.S. Army.

After Chisholm took up Black Beaver's old route, Chisholm's wagon tracts over Indian Territory were in turn followed by Texas cattle drovers when they first pushed their herds toward a railhead in Kansas in 1867.

That was when – probably unbeknownst to Jesse Chisholm – some trail boss, as his cowboys continued moving the cattle northward at some point after crossing the Red River, may have said:

"We'll just follow ol' Chisholm's trail."

Over a period of roughly 20 years – from the 1867 drives until just before the opening of the Unassigned Lands to settlement in 1889 – an estimated 4 to 6 million head of cattle were driven across present-day Oklahoma. In some places their hooves and chuck wagon wheels dug paths in the earth that remained visible well into the 21st century.

The name Chisholm was branded into history, and came to be applied not only to its stretch in present-day Oklahoma, but to the entire cattle trail, from deep in South Texas all the way to Abilene and later other railheads in Kansas.

And in fact, the "Chisholm Trail" – which has been called such things as "the world's greatest cattle trail" and the "high road of the cattle kingdom" – has even, mistakenly, in the minds of many, become the name of every cattle trail from Texas.

Chisholm, who may have been born in Tennessee and is believed to have grown up in present-day Arkansas among the Western Cherokees, came to be far more than a trader.

Historians have called him a multilingual scout, interpreter and peacekeeper between whites and Indians, and highly respected on the frontier that involved both Indian Territory and Texas.

It's believed that as an explorer, as well as a translator, guide and arbitrator for others, Chisholm traveled throughout much of the United States as well as Mexico.

According to Oklahoma historical writer Stan Hoig, Chisholm's diplomatic missions even included some to the office of U.S. President James Polk in Washington, where Chisholm interpreted during official visits by Indians; and he was a valuable aide to such dignitaries as U.S. Gen. Henry Leavenworth, Texas leader Sam Houston and Cherokee scholar Sequoyah – the latter to whom he may have been related.

Memories of Chisholm in Oklahoma also lingered for many years near the small McClain County town of Byars. Near there was Chisholm

Springs, where both Jesse Chisholm and a son, William, lived for a time; as well as the onetime community of Chism, named for William Chisholm.

Close to 140 years after Jesse Chisholm's death, a historical monument and what's left of his rugged gravestone briefly told the story of Chisholm and his death.

And, not far away was the Chisholm Trail Museum at Kingfisher – which was one of three in the state, the others being the Chisholm Trail Historical Museum at Waurika and the newest and largest, the Chisholm Trail Heritage Center at Duncan.

All three museums had been holding events at least once a year in recognizing various aspects of Jesse Chisholm's life and the Chisholm Trail.

Also, Yukon and other towns along the former trail had held annual or occasional Chisholm Trail festivals; and there had been several commemorative cattle drives, trail rides and wagon train jaunts under the name of Chisholm, originating both in Oklahoma and Texas.

And one was being planned for the state's Centennial Celebration in 2007 that was expected to be Oklahoma's biggest – a cattle drive from the Red River to Caldwell, Kansas, being organized by Ron Green of Jefferson.

Green, a cattleman and retired gas firm "pipeliner" in his middle 50s, said he hoped the drive, which would take about four weeks and cover some 240 miles in the late summer or fall, would be as authentic as possible.

Green had experience, having served as "trail boss" during a similar event in 1993.

In that commemorative Chisholm Trail jaunt, which was organized by Dr. Charlie Ogle, an Enid physician in his middle 50s, some 250 horseback riders and 10 chuck wagons took a herd of 300 cattle from Hennessey to Caldwell – a weeklong trip during which participants ate trail dust during the day and slept in wagons or on the ground at night.

However, if there was a single guru of Chisholm Trail history and lore, it was Robert L. "Bob" Klemme of Enid, a retired insurance man in his late 70s who has been entranced by the old trail since his junior high school days.

Over the years, he had virtually traced every foot of the old Chisholm Trail across Oklahoma – both close-up and via aerial photos

– plus from the Rio Grande near Brownsville, Texas, to Abilene, Kansas – and placed markers along much of the 1,000-mile stretch.

Also, Klemme, in partnership with Dr. Chris Jefferies of Duncan, a history teacher in his middle 60s who was former director of the Chisholm Trail Heritage Center there, was busy working to get the Chisholm designated as a national historic trail.

"Ever since a teacher told me about the Chisholm Trail, I've been fascinated by it," Klemme said. "The Chisholm Trail, you might say, is something that just kind of gets hold of ya."

Ghost Hollow (circa 1871) – Spooks and Gun Smoke

Ghost Hollow, a wooded vale near the Cimarron River in present-day Payne County, slightly north and east of central Oklahoma, is named for what's been described as a "curse" dating back to Indian Territory times, and its ensuing haunts over several decades.

Also, it's a ghost story enhanced by an unrelated but real-life incident. The hollow is in the general area of old Ingalls, the site of one of the biggest shoot-outs in the history of the Old West.

The name Ghost Hollow may date back to the early 1870s, when, according to stories, a young Indian woman was killed there when accidentally shot by her father.

 The legend has it that several other violent deaths occurred in that vicinity over the years, the period of doom extending to long after Oklahoma statehood. And all the macabre incidents supposedly resulted from the sad memory of the Indian girl's killing.

Lorraine Owens, who lived in Ingalls for several years, had repeated the legend of the "Indian princess" who angered her father when she tried to run off to marry a white man. The father, with either bow and arrow or gun, shot at the girl's suitor – but hit his fair daughter instead.

Afterwards, the story goes, in about 1888, three horse thieves were lynched in that area. Some years later a "crooked gambler" was strung up to the same tree. And over the years the region was the site of other unnatural deaths.

For many years the stories behind Ghost Hollow were especially entrancing because of two large trees that rubbed against one another when the wind blew. The eerie, moaning sounds spooked both humans and horses passing on the nearby road.

The town of Ingalls is where three officers and two bystanders died in a gun battle between federal lawmen and the Bill Doolin outlaw gang on Sept. 1, 1893.

Ingalls had begun with a post office on Jan. 22, 1890, in the Unassigned Lands of Indian Territory, which had been opened to settlement on April 22, 1889 – the event that would usher in the new Oklahoma Territory, created by the Organic Act of May 2, 1890.

That opening would become known as Oklahoma's first land run, or "land rush," and the Unassigned Lands would also be referred to as "Old Oklahoma."

Killed in the Ingalls shoot-out were U.S. deputy marshals Dick Speed, Tom Hueston and Lafayette "Lafe" Shadley, plus two townspeople shot by accident – N.A. Walker, who had been inside Ransom's Saloon, and Del Simmons, a teen-ager who was outside and running for cover when caught in the storm of bullets.

Bill Doolin and five of his gang escaped – though two were wounded, along with three bystanders.

Thundering out of town in a cloud of dust were Doolin, William "Tulsa Jack" Blake, George "Red Buck" Waightman, Alfred George "Bitter Creek" Newcomb, Dan "Dynamite Dick" Clifton and Bill Dalton.

Newcomb and Clifton had been hit, but could ride. Dalton's horse had been shot from under him, but he had jumped on behind Tulsa Jack.

The injured bystanders were saloon owner George Ransom, bartender Neil Murray and Frank Briggs, another teen-ager.

One of the outlaws, Roy Daugherty (also known as "Arkansas Tom" Jones), who had been firing from an upstairs window in the O.K. Hotel, finally surrendered and was hauled to jail.

Some 135 years after the supposed death of the Indian girl – and more than 112 years after the Ingalls shoot-out – one of the trees in Ghost Hollow had been removed, and its weird sounds were no longer heard.

Ingalls remained as a tiny, quiet community (its post office had closed in 1907), but with residents who liked tradition. Local folks were planning their next annual Ingalls Shoot-Out Re-enactment, held every September in conjunction with the local Old Settlers Reunion.

Gary Hennis, a 70-year-old Ingalls body shop operator and one of the area's main promoters, said the 1893 Ingalls shoot-out was remembered far more than the story of Ghost Hollow.

"You don't hear much about the place anymore," he said of the hollow, noting that it probably had something to do with the fact that someone had removed one of the two ancient trees there – either a sycamore or cottonwood – a few years earlier. "They were afraid it was going to fall on somebody, so they cut it down."

Apparently, the ghosts had left Ghost Hollow.

Cowboy Hill (circa 1871) – The Great 101

Cowboy Hill is a name that's been applied to what's left of one of Oklahoma's treasures: the Miller Brothers' 101 Ranch Wild West Show.

While the spot, on the south bank of the Salt Fork of the Arkansas River in northern Oklahoma, is only part of an area dedicated to the history of the once celebrated ranch and traveling exposition, many observers consider "Cowboy Hill" the symbolic heart of the old 101.

The 101 Ranch began as a grazing land for Texas longhorn cattle in Indian Territory and grew into an agricultural wonder, and finally a show that thrilled much of the world before it went broke some 60 years later.

During the time it was riding high, the 101 covered some 110,000 acres and was known as the "largest diversified farm and ranch in America."

Later as a show, with its multitudes of performing cowboys and Indians and its loads of animals, it journeyed throughout the nation and in Europe as one of the most spectacular attractions in history.

The ranch was founded by Col. George Washington Miller, a Confederate veteran from Kentucky, in the area of the Cherokee Outlet ("Cherokee Strip").

While not all historians agree on the year, it's believed the ranch began in the early 1870s when Miller leased land from the Indians — but that the land wasn't officially claimed until it was staked during the Sept. 16, 1893, land run that opened the Outlet to settlement.

The show was organized, at first for local performances, in about 1905 after Miller's sons — Joe, Zachary Taylor (or "Zack") and George L. – took over the ranch. It went "on the road" a few years later.

The ranch itself would become known for its buffalo as well as cattle, and even exotic animals, plus advanced agriculture experiments and animal crossbreeding. Along with its force of top-hand cowboys and other workers, it also had oil wells, and its own stores, blacksmith shops and about everything to make it virtually a small nation in itself.

The Miller family home, known as "the White House," hosted such visitors as onetime U.S. presidents Theodore "Teddy" Roosevelt and Warren G. Harding; military leaders Gen. John J. Pershing and Adm. Richard Byrd; national statesman William Jennings Bryan; Ameri-

The Cowboy Hill Cemetery

can newspaper magnate William Randolph Hearst; and boxing greats Jack Dempsey and Gene Tunney.

The show featured typical rodeo events such as rough stock riding, roping, trick-riding and fancy roping and shooting, plus other entertainment for all ages – ranging from terrapin racing (an attraction reportedly originated by the 101) to acts involving camels and elephants.

It attracted, as visitors if not participants, motion picture stars like Tom Mix – believed to have made his first movie there – Ken Maynard, Buck Jones and Hoot Gibson.

And the cowboys and cowgirls who made up the 101's entire troupe of performers over the years were almost without number.

It all came to an end when the ranch and show, beset with both economic and legal troubles, closed in 1931.

But memories of the great 101 have lingered over the years, enshrined by monuments and other physical reminders, and often revived by members of the 101 Ranch Old Timers Association and others.

The late Mike Sokoll is remembered as an early president of the Old Timers who hosted visitors to the 101 room in the Ponca City Cultural Center and taught rope tricks to youngsters.

Sokoll, who had finally settled in Ponca City, enjoyed telling how he was a descendant of Hungarian immigrants who joined the show as a runaway teen-ager from Pennsylvania. He said he was a cook's helper — "peeling spuds and such" — until becoming a trick roper, after being taught by veteran show member "Mexican Joe" Borrero.

In 1993, a Centennial Celebration of the 101 show, held at Ponca City's Marland Mansion and Estate, brought together hundreds of both veterans and fans of the one-time illustrious paragon of the American West.

Even a Tom Mix look-alike — S.A. "Tom" Darrigrand of Onsted, Michigan – showed up. Darrigrand, also a dedicated admirer of the onetime hard-riding actor and Oklahoma lawman, came not only in full Tom Mix regalia but with a horse to help impersonate his idol.

The celebration was inspired by Jerry Murphey of Corpus Christi, Texas, the grandson of Minnie Alemeda Murphey, once an Indian dancer with the show.

Memories were swapped all day by or about people like Murphey; Norma Shultz Ward of Guthrie, daughter of Charley Shultz, onetime clown with the show; Jack Webb, the show's fancy roper, trick roper and sharpshooter from California; and Jackie McFarland Laird of Ponca

City, one of the show's many cowgirl performers.

There also were a few stories, and talk of admiration, about Bill Pickett, the 101's black cowboy from Texas known for originating the sport of bulldogging a steer – and doing so by taking the critter's nose in his teeth.

Some of the former 101 cowhands or performers at the 1993 reunion were Sam Hill of Ponca City, Jack Quait of Newkirk and Buddy Kemp of Clarksville, Texas. Sitting under a shade tree, they talked and laughed about the old 101 – and how they missed it.

Hill said he went to work at the ranch when he was 14, and many years later still ached from riding broncs — but declared "I wouldn't change a damn thing."

Quait told how he "rode buckin' horses" and did trick riding, and spent his earnings "like a drunken sailor."

And when the show went broke, he said, "it was the saddest day of my life."

Kemp, also a former rough stock rider, recalled his days with the show when it traveled all over the country by rail.

"And if the train pulled out tomorrow," he said, "I'd be on it."

About 135 years after the reported beginning of the famous old ranch, Cowboy Hill remained among the 101 historical features on both sides of the river and in portions of both Kay and Noble counties. The overall historical area was a short distance north of Marland off State Highway 156.

Cowboy Hill itself, owned by the Oklahoma Historical Society, was the site of the graves of Zack Miller, Jack Webb and Sam Stigall, one of the ranch's original cowboys and a valued employee. Zack Miller had also given the hill to the Cherokee Strip Cow Punchers Association, a forerunner of the 101 Old Timers, as a site for their annual reunions.

The historical region also included remnants of the old White House and other structures of the ranch headquarters, designated as the 101 Ranch Historic District and on the National Register of Historic Places; and Monument Hill.

The latter, besides containing the monument to Ponca Chief White Eagle, was the site of Bill Pickett's grave, plus several unmarked graves believed to be of such 101 people as James "Curbstone Kirby" Smedley, who handled the show's oxen; cowboys Henry Horan and Henry Clay; Jim Gates, a farm hand who was killed in a bar fight; Gladys Hamilton, a ranch hand's young daughter who died in a house fire; a man known as "Old Charlie," believed to have been a cook; and a ranch worker known only as "Sailor."

Also buried there, apparently, was one of Bill Pickett's favorite horses, Croppy.

Jean Webb Evans of Marland, Jack Webb's daughter who was president of the Old Timers, said visitors from various places came regularly to the nearby 101 historical area.

Al Ritter of Ponca City, a longtime 101 historian and vice-president of the Old Timers as well as the author of a 101 Web site, was kept busy answering on-line questions.

Ritter, a retired Oklahoma state trooper in his late 50s, said numerous inquiries came from people whose relatives supposedly were with the 101 – "and ranging from helpers in the kitchen to workers who cleaned out stalls."

However, keeping records of people who were with the ranch and show wasn't easy, said John Cooper of Stroud, who was resident historian for the Old Timers.

For one thing, Cooper, a farmer in his middle 80s and a nephew of onetime 101 bulldogger Henry Cornett, said the show's performers "didn't have to give their real names."

"One might be 'Sam Jones' at one rodeo, and at the next place be somebody else," he said. "So you couldn't keep tract of all of 'em."

Ritter and Cooper agreed the name "Cowboy Hill" was an ideal representation of the history of the 101.

As to the origin of "101" itself, Cooper said reports vary.

One is that Miller branded his cattle on a horn, and some of one herd he bought had the brand of Bar-O-Bar – and in order to get all that on a horn, "he had to turn the bars up."

But another story has it that once when Miller bought some cattle in Texas that he planned to drive to a northern market, he had trouble getting his cowboys out of a local watering hole called the 101 Saloon.

So, Cooper said, Miller told his cowhands:

"If you like the name '101' so much, we'll brand the cattle that way. And you can look at it all the way to Kansas!"

Glass Mountains (1873) – 'Glassy' or 'Glossy'

The Glass Mountains, south of the Cimarron River in what is now Major County of northwestern Oklahoma, were given that name in 1873 when a government surveyor made a study for the U.S. General Land Office, according to early newspaper reports.

The land feature, in what was the previously mentioned Cherokee Strip, then in Indian Territory, was so called because the buttes contain selenite, or gypsum-type crystals that make them appear to contain bits of glass.

However, while the name on the 1873 survey reportedly was "Glass," the word "Gloss" showed up on a military map of that portion of the territory in 1875. And a controversy about the name has existed ever since.

One theory behind the issue is that a British surveyor gave his preferred pronunciation and spelling of the word. Another is that years ago when maps were hand-lettered, an "a" looked like an "o" – or maybe vice versa.

Regardless of how the disagreement started, some people – especially those in the vicinity of the land formation, near the small town of Orienta – have insisted "Gloss" is correct.

And partly because of this, according to the state Department of Transportation, the geological formation has, over a period of several years, been "on and off and on again" the official state map.

The mountains were on the state map – as "Glass" – during the years 1982 through 1985, but when Major County residents complained of that spelling, transportation officials threw up their hands and took the mountains off the map.

They were put back on the map – again as "Glass" – in 1996.

Then, for the 2005-06 map, they were still called "Glass Mountains" – but also with "Gloss" in parenthesis.

Close to 135 years after the reported survey that named the Glass Mountains, residents of the region remained proud of the chain of mesas that shimmer in the sunlight.

And, "Gloss" was still as imbedded in the local language as the shiny stuff was in the flat-toped hills.

There was a Gloss Mountain Conservancy, Inc., a volunteer non-profit group had been formed a few years earlier to further promote the land formation as a tourist attraction; as well as the Gloss Mountain State Park, a state project that was maintained by the conservancy.

There also was an event called the Gloss Mountains Cruisers' Car Show, held annually near Fairview.

At the Major County Historical Society in Fairview, Betty Harrison said "Gloss" was definitely a local name for the mountains:

"It's supposed to be 'Glass,' but they turned it into 'Gloss.'"

But she appeared to be the only person within miles who would say such a thing.

Mark Stubsten, chairman of the Gloss Mountain Conservancy, said that although a monument tells the story of the controversy of the name, the "Gloss" spelling is the hands-down winner in Major County.

"If you come here and ask anyone about that, they'll say the name is 'Gloss,'" said Stubsten, a Fairview banker and longtime resident of the area in his middle 50s.

He maintained books and various other data support the "Gloss" theory – "plus the fact that the locals want to say 'Gloss Mountains.'"

Bill Cornelsen, a rancher of nearby Cleo Springs in his late 40s, said his reasoning is simply the appearance of the mountains:

"I've always thought it was because they looked glossy."

Polecat Station (circa 1873) – Stages, Not Skunks

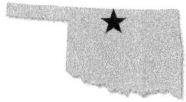

Polecat Station, which has been called the forerunner of the present-day town of Renfrow in Grant County of northern Oklahoma, may have acquired its name in the early 1870s as a stage stop in the Cherokee Strip of Indian Territory.

It apparently was a station operated by a firm called the "Southwestern Stage Coach Company" or "Southern Stage Company," established to haul mail and passengers from Caldwell, Kansas, southward toward Fort Sill.

The station was named for nearby Polecat Creek (also called "Pole Cat Creek").

That area was also the location of a Pole Cat Ranch – which, according to one story, in the 1880s was where two cowboys, while temporarily living in a dugout, were awaken one night by a wild critter that had entered their small abode. And they had to use their six-shooters to evict the invader — a large cougar.

Nearly 135 years after the surmised beginning of Polecat Station, the site of the place was believed to be in a wheat field a few miles southeast of Renfrow. And about all that was left of the old stage stop, according to the owner of the property, Louis Skirdla, were "pieces of an old cook stove and things of that nature."

Skirdla, a farmer in his middle 60s, speculated the site first became known during the early years of the Chisholm Trail, but said he didn't know the full history of the region — "just that this was along the old trail where they drove the cattle, and they bedded 'em down on the south side of the creek."

As to the reason for the "polecat" name in the first place, he had no idea. He said his part of the state wasn't especially known for skunks – any more so than it was for cougars.

Hennessey (1874) – The Ambush

Hennessey, in present-day Oklahoma's Kingfisher County, is significant because it was named for the victim of one of the violent and tragic events on the American frontier.

Despite the variance in spelling, the town traces its beginning to what's been called the "Hennessy Massacre" on July 4, 1874, in what was then part of Indian Territory.

On that date, which was Saturday, Pat Hennessy, a native of Ireland who was a wagon freighter on the Chisholm Trail, was ambushed and killed, his body mutilated and burned, apparently by renegade Indians.

The attack occurred at or near the site of the town that would be named for him – and where, it is believed, he would be buried.

The town of Hennessey's post office – at first with the spelling of "Hennesy" — opened on July 20, 1889, in the previously mentioned Unassigned Lands of Indian Territory, which would become Oklahoma Territory the next year.

For several years, the attack on Pat Hennessy's wagon train, based on research by the late Tom G. McGee, a Kingfisher County educator, was re-enacted in an annual pageant by local actors.

It was presented in 1939 and several more times until being replaced by an annual "Pat Hennessy Celebration" – with virtually no reference to the man's tragic death. Even that event was discontinued in the early 1990s.

Hennessy is honored by a Pat Hennessey Memorial Garden, which in 1941 was provided for the community by local poet Annette B. Ehler.

A few days before that fateful July 4 of 1874, Pat Hennessy, 37 and unmarried, had left the office of the Laflerie freighting company near Wichita, Kansas, in charge of three wagons, each drawn by a team of six mules and loaded mostly with grain, sugar and coffee. They were heading south, for the Comanche, Kiowa and Apache Agency in the area of Fort Sill.

With him were two other drivers, George Fant and Thomas Calloway, and a passenger and helper, Ed Cook.

When their bodies were found, scattered over some distance, they all had been scalped and mutilated.

One report said Hennessy "had been burned alive . tied to his wagon and burned," his body "still roasting in the fire."

It's been argued – at least by Ehler, who designed the local monument – that Hennessy was killed by white men masquerading as Indians.

However, conventional reports indicate the evidence at the scene of the slaying supports the theory of an Indian attack.

Also, historians say it was during a time when Indians in that area were said to be hungry, and angry. The land was in a severe summer drought, and the Cheyenne, Arapaho, Kiowa, Comanche and Apache Indians, as well as some Osages, had to survive where little game was left and farming was difficult, and on goods that were hauled in.

Also, it was reported that Cheyenne-Arapaho Agent John D. Miles at Darlington had unsuccessfully appealed for military help from Washington, both to control Indians and to protect them from white horse thieves and other outlaws – another major cause of Indian restlessness.

More than 130 years after Pat Hennessy's slaying, the town of Hennessey was expected to revive the commemoration of his death, and to stage the event in September of 2007, Oklahoma's centennial year.

Jean Ann Casey, representing the 2010 Committee, which served as Hennessey's chamber of commerce, said it would probably be called the "Pat Hennessy Massacre Re-Enactment." While details were yet to be worked out, she said, "we're definitely going to do something."

Hennessey resident Bob Lovell, a retired Kingfisher County associate district judge in his late 70s who was among local historians, said he expected the renewed pageant to be appreciated, especially by younger people.

"When you've got a new generation, they'll rise to the occasion," he said.

Meanwhile, Mary Haney, local library director, said various exhibits and programs at the library were aimed at educating people that the local tragedy was part of a violent era in the history of the entire Southwest.

"We're trying to show them, especially the children, the whole of it – the Red River Wars and all that," she said. "We want to keep it in front of their eyes."

As for Pat Hennessy himself, she said, "He's not forgotten."

Pat Hennessy Park and grave marker in Hennessey.

Doan's Crossing (circa 1874) – The Great Western

Doan's Crossing – its former site being in present-day Jackson County of southwestern Oklahoma – was a stopping place along the Great Western cattle trail that was on the north side of the Red River, in what was then Texas.

Believed to have consisted of a corral and a shack or two, Doan's Crossing probably came into being when cattle were first driven up the trail in 1874, and existed until the trail closed in about 1895.

The Doan's Crossing on the north side of the river – which for several years was part of the aforementioned Greer County, Texas - possibly was smaller, and lesser known, than the Doan's Crossing that was a large holding area on the river's south side, in Texas proper. Both places were named for merchant C.F. Doan.

The Great Western Trail – which also was called such names as the Dodge City Trail and the Texas Trail – pretty well replaced the previously described Chisholm Trail, several miles to the east. The Chisholm, which opened in 1867, had begun to dwindle in the number of cattle when drovers began using the Great Western. The Chisholm was officially closed by 1889.

More than 130 years after Doan's Crossing was believed to have been established, little remained of the place on the north side of the river; and overall, the Great Western Trail itself was said to be shy of historical recognition – although a group of Oklahomans were doing something about that.

Several area residents were working with the local Western Trail Historical Society to place markers along the old cattle trail, from the Doan's Crossing location, near Hess, all the way north to Kansas. The distance is about 200 miles.

A monument had been dedicated at the old Doan's Crossing a few years earlier, and the concrete indicators were still being placed, said John Yudell Barton, who helped direct the project.

Others in the Oklahoma venture included Mike McAskill, a rancher of about 60 who owned the Doan's Crossing land. His grandfather, Dan J. Briscoe, once worked at the store at the Doan's Crossing on the Texas side.

The southwestern Oklahoma group felt like the Great Western for several years had been in the historical and cultural shadow of the Chisholm Trail – both in the state, where it's portrayed by three museums, and nationally.

The group even talked of establishing a "Great Western Trail Museum" in Altus – or at least adding a special wing to the local Museum of the Western Prairie.

That museum's curator, Bart McClenny, decried the attitude of many museum visitors who, upon hearing the mention of the local cattle trail, would say, 'Oh, yes, the Chisholm Trail!'"

Barton, a retired Altus pharmacist in his early 70s who called himself "an interested drugstore cowboy," said the local effort was paying off.

For one thing, he said, it had inspired people in Texas to install trail markers also; and several trail riders and teamsters from Bandera had recently come through Oklahoma with the theme of "Celebrate the Western Trail."

"It seems like we've started all this," Barton said.

"And now we're working on Kansas."

Needmore (circa 1875) – Not Short of Memories

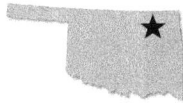

Needmore is said to have started in 1875 with a small store in the valley of the Neosho, or Grand, River in the Cherokee Nation of Indian Territory, in present-day Delaware County of northeastern Oklahoma, at the edge of Grand Lake O' the Cherokees.

And while it's uncertain exactly when, or how, the place was named, it's believed it came from a remark about its less-than-prosperous condition long before its post office was established on Dec. 14, 1894.

However, the farming trade center apparently thrived for some 18 years until the town of Bernice was settled nearby – and Needmore became better known as Bernice, whose post office opened in 1913.

About 130 years after Needmore's supposed beginning, virtually its only reminder was the Rolston Cemetery – named for one of its pioneers – on a strip of land known as Monkey Island. The site of old Needmore was nearby.

And ironically, the region certainly didn't appear hard-up.

Rose Stauber of Grove, a researcher for the Delaware County Genealogical Society, described Monkey Island as the scene of "a very high influx of retirees," and with no sign at all of a bad economy. "That's all long gone," she said.

Norma Jean Hensley of near Afton, who had lived in the Bernice area for some 70 years, agreed that the region had "some beautiful homes down in there, and a nice restaurant, a golf course and all."

Connie Cook, a Grove real estate broker, called the former Needmore area "a big vacation spot now, like many of the lake places – with some pretty high-dollar condominiums and other things there."

But years ago, according to stories, it was different.

It's said that Louis Rolston Jr., from Georgia, and his wife, Eliza, came to the Needmore area with little more than a team of oxen and $5 in cash – and that he got the money on the way, as a reward for saving a woman traveler when her buggy overturned in a flooded stream.

Needmore's first school was described as a one-room affair, and with the teacher being paid by one or two dollars that each child would bring each month — hopefully.

Norma Jean Hensley said her family's modest home, like many others during their move to Bernice, was hauled from Needmore.

"My folks bought that house for sixty-five dollars," she said. "We were all poor in those days."

Doug Klaus of Afton, a retired tire company employee in his late 60s, said the Needmore area had considerable poverty for years after the town's official demise.

"It was real poor," he said. "I remember Mama making water gravy for breakfast."

Not that the community's economic picture was all bleak – or that the people were without grit.

It was reported that the late Gove Bunch, who spent most of his life in the Needmore-Bernice area and once was town treasurer of Bernice, said during the early 1940s of the town's progress:

"We have not received a single government or state subsidy to expand our facilities. What we have today is the result of residents digging down in their pockets."

And Needmore was a fine place to live, recalled 102-year-old Thelma Muskrat Lee, a former longtime resident and historian of Needmore who was living in the Oklahoma Methodist Manor in Tulsa.

"I remember Needmore, and the people of Needmore," she said. "They were nice people – well-respected people and very nice people."

But that's all gone, she said. "There's nothing left of Needmore."

Trail (circa 1875) – Horses and Trains

Trail, in present-day Dewey County of western Oklahoma, began as a stop along the Great Western cattle trail on the south side of the Canadian River in the Cheyenne and Arapaho lands of Indian Territory.

It was believed to have started as a small business — the Trail Store – in about 1875, and moved for a short distance before its post office opened on June 18, 1898, in what had then become Oklahoma Territory.

After its post office closed in 1929, it survived for many years as a tiny community, and would be remembered by some because of the cattle trail.

Harry Jones, an early-day rancher of Camargo, nearby but north of the river, when in his middle 80s had passed along stories of how a small boy once stood and watched, "and it took hours and hours and hours for the cattle to go by."

But there were many more memories about Trail during the 1900s – how it eventually became a farming and ranching center along State Highway 34 as well as the MK&T (Katy) Railroad, until the rail service was discontinued.

And many of the stories involved both the railroad and horses.

It was told by some area residents that young people of Trail, when going to dances at Camargo, would cross the river on the railroad bridge, which was about three-fourths of a mile long.

And they had to walk — unless they caught a ride on a particular, sure-footed horse.

It was said the horse – a large animal named Roan – would calmly and carefully step on the spaced railroad ties high above the water until it got safely across the river.

"Sometimes a bunch of kids would ride that horse," Dorothy Schandorf Peters of Camargo once said. "It'd make several trips a night."

Lee Craig, a Trail resident in his late 70s, had once told similar stories about the horse taking young people across the river:

"They could ride both with saddle and bareback, and sometimes there'd be one in saddle and one or two behind – and someone else holding to its tail and walkin'."

Other times, people rode horses across the river by either fording it when it was low or by swimming the horses across when it was up, according to Dorothy Peters – and that reminded her of another unusual horse story.

She said her brother, Gene Schandorf, had a horse, Max, that served as free public transportation in the area of both Trail and Camargo. Anyone could ride it, and it would then come home by itself.

Late one night, she said, Max had already been ridden by a few people back and forth from Trail to Camargo – when at Camargo, a man from Trail had car trouble and was worried about getting home.

"But then he saw that horse come walkin' down the road," Dorothy said. So the man got on, rode across the river and went home to Trail.

Max didn't get finished transporting people until the next day, she said. "The horse finally got home about noon."

Some 130 years after the estimated beginning of Trail, about all that was left of the town was a grain elevator and a few old foundations. But it remained on the latest official state map, and still had an identity.

James Craig, a native of the area in his early 80s who was retired from the oil fields, said he had doubts about some of the local reminiscing – "you can find yourself one of these benches and get a plug of chewin' tobacco, and hear a lot of stories."

However, he had his own special memories about Trail during the time it was served by the railroad.

"The train would stop and let you get on right here at Trail," he said, and he recalled a particular time when he and pretty Leojenne Fegel took a trip some 60 years before:

"My wife and I got on the train here and went to Woodward to get married."

Sacred Heart (circa 1875) – A Mission and Mystery Books

Sacred Heart, possibly founded as a mission as early as the fall of 1875 in the Pottawatomie and Shawnee lands, then in Indian Territory, symbolizes the establishment of the Catholic faith in the territory. It's been called "the Cradle of Oklahoma Catholicism."

As a community, Sacred Heart, in present-day Pottawatomie County, a short distance southeast of the center of the state, is also the native home of nationally known mystery writer Tony Hillerman, who became a longtime resident of Albuquerque, New Mexico.

As Sacred Heart Mission, historical records say it was officially established in 1876 by two French Benedictine monks, Father Isidore Robot and Brother Dominic Lambert, to teach the Catholic principles to the Indians and settlers in that area. However, records also say the monks began their work there in October 1875.

The ministry soon became the nucleus for St. Gregory's University at Shawnee, which has been called the oldest institution of higher learning in present-day Oklahoma. Historians say its first classes were taught there in 1915.

Sacred Heart Mission's post office opened on Jan. 30, 1879, and its name was changed to Sacred Heart on May 24, 1888. The post office closed in 1954.

About 130 years after it was named, Sacred Heart, off State Highway 39 about six miles east of Asher, consisted of the Church of the Sacred Heart and the Immaculate Conception, commonly known as "Sacred Heart Church" – an impressive structure dating back to 1914 and the core of the tiny community – the home of the pastor, Father Matthew Brown; a historical marker; a cemetery; and a few homes.

Also, at the bottom of a hill in a tranquil area amid a pasture of grazing cattle, were the ruins of the old mission. A few homes were nearby.

The church apparently was still a popular place – with both visitors from faraway and residents, local people said.

"It's quiet and peaceful here, and that church is beautiful, especially on the inside," said Steve Matthew, a man in his late 40s who lived a short distance away. "We walk up there a lot and look around."

Kathy DeLonais Lowry, who grew up in Sacred Heart and lived at nearby Konawa, said she and husband Tim, who was president of the Sacred Heart Historical Society, kept in regular touch with the community as well as the church.

She noted her great-grandfather, Francis DeLonais, helped build the church, and her parents, James and Norma DeLonais, once had a store there.

Noting that hers wasn't the only French name, she said that "a lot of different heritages have come together here – the French, the Pottawatomie Indians, of course, and others — I think it's sort of a 'melting pot' of Oklahoma."

She also said Hillerman, although his home was many miles away, was still considered a Sacred Heart resident. "He comes and visits once in a while, and once he was talking about things around Sacred Heart, like the old cotton gin — that I remember, too."

She added: "And he signed one of his books for me!"

Wauhillau (circa 1879) – Ned and a Water Mill

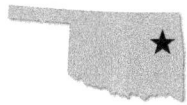

Wauhillau, a rural area in present-day Adair County of eastern Oklahoma, apparently began in the late 1870s in the Cherokee Nation of Indian Territory. Its post office opened on Feb. 13, 1879.

The place is remembered for its pretty name – believed to be from a Cherokee word, Awa'hili, meaning "eagle" — but also for being near the site of a monumental battle in 1892 between about a dozen lawmen and alleged Cherokee outlaw Ned Christie.

While the story about Christie is controversial, he was wanted as a criminal when the posse dynamited him out of his log fort on the rim of a canyon after a two-day standoff. As he ran from the blazing ruins, he was killed in a storm of bullets.

Wauhillau is also where an authentic water mill for grinding corn, operated by Golda Unkefer and called Golda's Old Stone Milling Co., became a thriving tourist business during the 1950s.

For a time the mill, powered by the clear stream known as Bitting Springs, attracted busloads of tourists, and even movie stars. And part of one movie, "Where the Red Fern Grows," was filmed there.

More than 125 years after Wauhillau's beginning, the area was a quiet place where two picturesque lakes were fed by Bitting Springs.

The area also included the farm homes of Loretta Dickson and her son, Levi. Her late husband, George, had once helped operate the mill.

The post office had closed in 1935. One wheel was left of the old mill, which had burned in 1983. Golda Unkefer had long been deceased.

Visitors interested in the old water mill were virtually nil compared to those many years before.

Golda's Mill, like Ned Christie, was virtually forgotten.

Robbers Cave (circa 1880) – Belle's Abode?

Robbers Cave, one of present-day Oklahoma's most remarkable natural attractions, may have acquired its captivating name long before law-abiding tourists would hear of it.

Robbers Cave State Park, near Wilburton in Latimer County of southeastern Oklahoma, was established in 1926 as a remote camp, finally becoming a state park in 1935. It's believed it was known by such early names as Camp Tom Hale and Cave Springs.

However, regardless of park reports, some historians believe the cave could have been unofficially named as early as 1880 when it was part of Indian Territory – which at that time was crawling with bad characters who often needed a place to hide.

Since 1875, deputies had been hunting down wanted criminals in most of present-day Oklahoma for Isaac "Hanging Judge" Parker at Fort Smith, the U.S. judge of the Western District of Arkansas, with jurisdiction over all of Indian Territory.

It's believed the cave, among rugged cliffs and with even a nearby natural rock corral, would somehow be described by the lawmen as an ideal spot for bad men to hole up – and maybe not just men.

According to legend, another person who frequented the area was Belle Starr, a flashy gal with a liking for riding good horses and wearing two pistols, but with little love for the law.

While she wasn't as bad as her dime-novel reputation – which earned her such nicknames as "The Bandit Queen," "The Lady Desperado," "Wild Woman of the Wild West" and "Petticoat Terror of the Plains" — she hung out with and aided outlaws, and was proud of it.

It's believed Belle was in the territory a few years before 1880, after her first husband, outlaw Jim Reed, was killed in Texas. She lived in Younger's Bend, a canyon area about a day's ride from the cave.

She spent about nine months in prison, for horse stealing – her only criminal conviction, though she was linked with several villainous acts.

Her life ended in 1889 when she was shot off her horse from ambush — a murder that went unsolved.

More than 125 years after the supposed naming of Robbers Cave, the state park by that name remained popular, said assistant manager Merle Cox – especially, he said, among visitors from other places, who he said "think this is an unusually beautiful part of the country."

However, for many area natives, Robbers Cave State Park was simply another name for Belle Starr.

And some, it seemed, had known her.

Kay Shero of Wilburton frequently donned a black velvet riding habit or similar garb and did personal portrayals of Belle, often in the park.

She said her audiences "love to hear about Belle."

And Kay loved to talk about Belle.

"I used to think of her as pretty wild, but she was a woman of her time," Shero said. "She did the best she could with what life presented her."

Bobbie Vinson, also of Wilburton, had similar sentiments:

"She did what she had to do to make a living. And she got in trouble because of who she was married to."

Gene Foster, a Wilburton native who lived in Muskogee, also enjoyed discussing Belle.

"She and her boyfriend, or whatever he was, would hide in Robbers Cave," he said. "And once they were inside, with a natural corral and lookouts and all, the law couldn't do much to 'em."

Foster, a 60-year-old retired technician for a utility firm, figured stories like that inspired the name of what finally became a famous park:

"It all started with Belle Starr."

Oklahoma (1881) — An OK Idea!

Oklahoma — probably before anyone imagined it would become the name of a state — began as a small town in the Choctaw Nation of Indian Territory in 1881, its post office established on Dec. 21 of that year.

It marked the first official use of the word, which nine years later would become the name of Oklahoma Territory, and 26 years later, the name of the 46th state of the Union.

The location of the town of Oklahoma would later be part of Haskell County in the eastern part of the state.

However, its name was changed to Whitefield on Nov. 27, 1888, to avoid confusion with Oklahoma Station, whose post office had been opened in 1887.

The name Oklahoma, which is Choctaw for "Red People," apparently was suggested in the 1860s by the previously mentioned Rev. Allen Wright. It was said the Choctaw leader proposed the name for a new territory "of the Indian people" — although such a territory was never officially organized.

Some historians have wondered whether Wright, who died in 1885, would consider it a consolation that the name would designate the new Oklahoma Territory in 1890 – and 17 years later, when Indian Territory and Oklahoma Territory united, the state of Oklahoma.

The word, along with the 1931 play by Claremore writer Lynn Riggs, "Green Grow the Lilacs," also inspired and became the name of the early 1940s musical by Rodgers and Hammerstein, "Oklahoma!"

That in turn became the state's official song — which to Oklahomans is right up there with the National Anthem.

About 125 years after the beginning of the town of Oklahoma, Whitefield, at the crossroads of two state highways, was a place of about 230 residents.

However, the mayor, Harold Alverson, a retired carpenter in his late 60s, said the town had been growing in recent years, but that the business district was still comprised of "two stores and a junk dealer – we call it 'the Whitefield Wal-Mart.'"

Noretta Livesay, president of the Haskell County Historical Society in nearby Stigler, said it seemed that few area residents were aware that Whitefield once had the name of Oklahoma.

"In a small town it gets to the point where the old-timers have died away and the young people have moved away to make a living, and history gets lost," she said. "It's sad, but that's the way it is."

Glenn Hyder, a writer in his middle 50s who also was with the historical society, agreed, saying Whitefield folks talked far less about their town's "Oklahoma" background than about "Belle Starr's ghost."

He referred to the fact that it was near Whitefield that the so-called Bandit Queen was shot off her horse and killed by an unknown assassin one Sunday in 1889 – the beginning of a legend that says her image appears on nights of a full moon.

Hyder figured that was the local peoples' brand of Oklahoma history.

Wetumka (1881) – A Bunch of Suckers

Wetumka officially began when its post office opened on Feb. 1, 1881, in the Creek Nation of Indian Territory, and eventually became a town in Hughes County in the eastern half of Oklahoma.

It's remembered partly because of its interesting name – apparently from a Creek word meaning "tumbling water" – but far better known because of its self-proclaimed slogan, "Sucker Capital of the World."

Wetumka – though not intentionally – would become famous after a smooth-talking stranger who called himself F. Bam Morrison appeared in the quiet little town one day in 1950 and said he was making preparations for a local circus performance. The big tent entourage would arrive soon, he promised, and it would be the biggest event in Wetumka's history.

For several days the whole town was full of anticipation, until local merchants – after spending an estimated $3,000 on hot dog wieners, soda pop and truckloads of hay (for the elephants), along with living expenses for F. Bam Morrison – realized that no circus was coming.

And, that F. Bam Morrison was gone.

They had been hornswoggled, and the swindle was definitely the

biggest event in Wetumka's history.

The town was left with all the food and other fixings for the circus – plus a bunch of red faces and people swearing how they wish they could find and tar and feather F. Bam Morrison.

But when tempers cooled, town fathers had an idea. What the heck, circus or no circus, since they were prepared for a good time, why not produce one of their own? And at least get rid of all the hot dogs and soda pop?

They scheduled a big local festival, and planned to hold it every year.

And when they considered what to call it, someone said "Well, he did make *suckers* out of us, so ..."

Ever since then, "Sucker Day" has been Wetumka's regular celebration, held annually except for a few misses.

It's brought in thousands of visitors and been a boon to the local economy, plus one of Oklahoma's most publicized events. Over the years it's even gained international recognition.

"Sucker Day put Wetumka on the map!" an ecstatic town booster once declared.

One story has it that Wetumkans became so jubilant over the festival's success — and so magnanimous and even appreciative in their feelings toward F. Bam Morrison – that they wanted to invite him to serve as parade marshal in the next annual Sucker Day.

It was said they finally located him — in jail someplace in Missouri. And he agreed to come to the celebration – *if* they would send him bail and travel money first.

They found someone else to be parade marshal.

Some 125 years after Wetumka's beginning, and more than 55 years after the start of its Sucker Day tradition, Wetumka remained a quiet, friendly community, and plans were being made for the next big celebration, expected to be sometime in September.

Bill Morgan, editor of the local *The Hughes County Times* newspaper, said the town, as usual, was expected to be jam-packed on the big day.

"It's amazing how many people come back for that every year," said Morgan, a man in his middle 70s and a dedicated promoter of the celebration.

In fact, he was the one who said Sucker Day put the town on the map.

Dead Indian Lake (circa 1881) – Non-politically Right

Dead Indian Lake, in Rogers Mills County of western Oklahoma, possibly came from a term used by white settlers in the early 1880s in the aforementioned Cheyenne and Arapaho lands, at that time still in Indian Territory.

It's been speculated that Dead Indian Creek was named when settlers discovered the body of an Indian that, following the custom of some tribes, had been laid to rest on a burial scaffold of cottonwood limbs in the vicinity of the stream.

The creek apparently has been called Dead Indian ever since, and so has the nearby lake after it was created when a dam was built in the 1950s.

That is, until the late 1990s when a Norman woman complained to the U.S. Board on Geological Names that the name of the lake, which is on part of the Black Kettle National Grassland, was offensive. And she asked that it be changed.

Some state groups agreed, but as soon as a new sign for "Black Kettle Lake" was put up, several western Oklahomans, headed by Leona Keahey of near Crawford — a lifelong resident of about two miles from the lake — protested the change. Leona claimed to have a petition of about 1,200 names, of both non-Indians and Indians.

Also, her group financed two nearly billboard-sized "Dead Indian Lake" signs on private land along U.S. Highway 283.

Around 125 years after the supposed naming of Dead Indian Creek, the eight-year squabble over the name had calmed, but remained unsettled, with names and signs in a muddle of confusion.

Both the federal agency and the Oklahoma Board on Geographic Names had become involved, and the U.S. board was expected to consider the matter again.

However, one official observer said the problem appeared to have "no satisfactory solution."

And the Norman woman who first complained about the name – Maria Protti – had moved to California, and officials handling the case had been unable to contact her.

The large "Dead Indian Lake" signs instigated by Leona Keahey had been taken down, because of property concerns.

However, one had been put back up, with a rancher's permission – but then was blown down during a storm. So Leona paid someone (out of donations) who was going to put it up again.

But in the meantime she was worried, since she said it was "down in the canyon, and a cow could step on it or something."

Leona, a hearty woman in her middle 80s, also remained upset over the whole issue, claiming that historical names, like history itself, shouldn't be changed:

"It's like 'Native Americans' – they know they're Indians!"

Among her allies was Gary Turley of Yukon, a retired salesman in his middle 60s and a native of Cheyenne. He called the proposed name change "all politics – this is definitely 'political correctness.'"

Meanwhile, at the entrance to the nearby lake, a sign read "Black Kettle Recreation Area." And on at least one state map, in the *Oklahoma Atlas & Gazetteer,* the reservoir was labeled "Black Kettle Lake."

However, where the 283 highway crosses the stream that is the heart of the argument, the sign "Dead Indian Creek" remained.

At the Black Kettle Museum in Cheyenne, museum consultant Virginia Reynolds said when visitors heard the subject mentioned, "sometimes there's a little grin, and sometimes there isn't."

And it seemed the people least vocal about the whole thing were the area's Indians.

Glena Belle Crane, a retired teacher in her 90s living in Cheyenne, said she had many Indian friends.

"And they're proud," she said, but when the issue about the lake's name arose, "they didn't give a hoot."

Paw Paw (1882) – 'Way Down Yonder...'

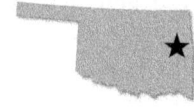

Paw Paw, in present-day Sequoyah County of eastern Oklahoma, began as a town on the bank of the Arkansas River when its post office opened on Dec. 26, 1882, in the Cherokee Nation of Indian Territory.

The place is remembered for its unusual name – which brings to some minds the title of a favorite old song. The town was situated in what was called Paw Paw Bottom, where it was believed many paw-paw trees grew at one time.

However, some reports indicate the place was named for a secret organization of Southern sympathizers that existed during the Civil War.

Paw Paw is also known by historians as a town that was virtually destroyed by the once-volatile river. It remained as a farming community for several years after its post office closed in 1915 – but finally was virtually wiped out by two major floods, in 1927 and in 1943.

Years afterward, both good and bad times were recalled by former resident Howard Watts.

He told of outdoor gatherings when families had picnics and sang "Way Down Yonder in the Pawpaw Patch."

Of the floods, he said that while no lives were lost, the raging waters had swept away cattle, horses and hogs, and caused homes to "cave off into the river."

He said the first flood he remembered, in 1927, nearly devastated the community – then the river's rampage in 1943 "made the 1927 flood look like the mornin' dew."

Nearly 125 years after the beginning of Paw Paw, the only sign of the community, south of Muldrow, was its cemetery.

Virginia Falkner said she and her husband, Jim, a retired factory worker in his early 60s, lived "just on the edge of Paw Paw Bottom," but seldom heard comments about its name.

But she also said that since the nearby McClellan-Kerr Arkansas River Navigation System had brought about flood control, they were glad they didn't have to worry about getting washed away.

Tin City (circa 1883) — Prairie Patchwork

Tin City started out as the tackiest post office in Texas and finally became Mangum, Oklahoma.

At least, that's one description of the little store that was the hub of an early-day settlement.

It was established in the early 1880s in what was then the aforesaid Greer County, Texas. It became Mangum when the post office of that name opened on April 15, 1886 – 21 years before it would become part of southwestern Oklahoma.

The store was opened by Henry Sweet, a Texas surveyor hired by Captain A.S. Mangum, who had been given the land by Texas as a reward for his military service, apparently in the Mexican-American War.

The mercantile center, as the first public building there, also was where settlers could pick up their mail — brought in by horseback from the Texas town of Quanah.

It's believed the words "Tin City" were first voiced by cowboys, who would ride by the store and laugh.

One historical report says the store was a log structure that had been moved there – "and the cracks between the logs were covered with tin cans that had been opened and straightened out." It's believed the cans originally came from the store's stock of canned peaches and tomatoes.

Close to 125 years after the beginning of Tin City, its site was believed to be in the middle of Mangum.

"I don't know the exact location, but I'm sure it was somewhere here in the square," said local postmaster Judy Forehand.

Peggy Bielich, a local history enthusiast, said that on the prairie, "lumber was very difficult to come by, and what they used had to be hauled in from Quanah."

So, she said, tin cans apparently made sense to Sweet – "especially back during the time when he started that store-like thing."

And according to Curtis Bell of nearby Reed, the cans probably worked.

Bell, a rancher in his middle 50s and known as a cowboy poet, explained it all in a few words:

"They had to figure some way to stop that old wind."

Keokuk Falls (circa 1888) – Jim Thorpe

Keokuk Falls, once a bustling and rowdy settlement near the North Fork of the Canadian River in the Sac and Fox lands of Indian Territory, apparently began in the late 1880s when Henry C. Jones, a half Sac and Fox, opened a store near some picturesque falls on the river.

The site is in present-day Pottawatomie County, and near the river that came to be officially called the North Canadian.

The town apparently boomed when the reservation was opened to white settlement in 1891, and was officially named – for Moses Keokuk, a Sac and Fox chief — when its post office opened Jan. 13, 1892.

Keokuk Falls is known as the home of onetime world famous American Indian athlete Jim Thorpe, who was born near there in 1887.

It's also remembered for its reputation as one of the wildest and toughest places on the Western frontier.

Following the 1890 creation of Oklahoma Territory, it was situated roughly on the border of the Indian and Oklahoma territories – with alcoholic drink banned in one place and sold openly in the other – and for a time was called "the drinking capital of the Indian country."

Liquor and beer were sold all over town, night and day. It was said that even hogs, after feeding on mash in an alley back of a distillery, would stagger down the main street next to the human drunks.

Jim Thorpe, who grew up to win both the decathlon and pentathlon and several medals in the 1912 Olympic Games in Sweden — to be called the "World's Greatest Athlete" — lived near Keokuk as a youngster, according to Jim's daughters, Grace and Gail.

Grace also said Jim's father, Hiram, who raised horses in the area, did his share of whooping it up in Keokuk Falls.

"Grandpa Thorpe," she said, often would spend several hours in the town's saloons, and when driving his hack out of town, "he'd have both pistols out and would shoot out the lights."

Nearly 120 years after the apparent beginning of Keokuk Falls, about the only sign of the place was a historical marker in the vicinity that designated the area as the home of Jim Thorpe. Its post office had closed in 1918.

Jim Burch, a rancher in his late 50s who lived nearby, noted that the region was quiet and peaceful – a drastic change from the way history described it in its heyday.

"That's been so long ago, all that's hard to believe," he said. "Now, there's nothing there. Nothing."

Beer City (circa 1888) – A State Line Tradition

Beer City, in what finally became the northwestern corner of Beaver County in the Oklahoma Panhandle, was a place in No Man's Land where cowboys whooped it up.

It's believed it began in the late 1880s when tents and a few shacks blossomed as saloons, dance halls, gambling houses and the like.

The center of sin, so to speak – also called White City, apparently because of the many tents gleaming on the sunny plains – supplied entertainment to men brought to the region by the cattle trade and the railroad in nearby Kansas.

Especially because of its proximity to Kansas — where drinking and similar activity were frowned upon – Beer City was wide open and wicked until 1890 when the Panhandle became part of Oklahoma Territory, and more lawful.

But during Beer City's short life, patrons reportedly found recreation in the Elephant Saloon and other joints such as the Yellow Snake, where Pussy Cat Nell, a madam, ran a thriving business upstairs.

It was said that during the busy cattle-shipping season, women were imported from Kansas, with hack loads of them coming in at regular times from Liberal.

And at night that part of the Panhandle was aglow with red lights.

Close to 120 years after Beer City began, the name still intrigued history buffs and tourists, said Debbie Colson, director of the No Man's Land Museum in Goodwell.

"I think it was almost another Dodge City (Kansas)," she said. "It had to do with the cattle trade, and when you have cattle you have cowboys, and when you have cowboys you have all the other."

And roughly on the site of old Beer City, north of Turpin along U.S. Highway 83 and barely south of the Kansas state line, was a spot of civilization with no particular name.

But compared to the rowdy place that once was there, it was plumb peaceful. Apparently, its most exciting attraction was the State Line Bingo.

There also was a Mexican-style dance hall, *El Potrero* ("the Colt Corral"), a café and a drive-in place called Gladys' Beer and Cigarette Outlet.

And one might consider Gladys' the epitome of the small community, since it existed for the same reason, to a degree, that old Beer City did.

Bob Farris, a local resident in his middle 50s who operated Farris Well Service across the line in Liberal, said his community was nice and quiet, "but places like bars will always be there — because of the Sunday deal."

In other words, while the situation there wasn't nearly like it was around 120 years before, over in Kansas you still couldn't buy beer on Sundays – and on the Oklahoma side, you had no problem.

Nowata (1889) – A Dry Place?

Nowata, in present-day northeastern Oklahoma and the seat of Nowata County, was officially established on Nov. 8, 1889, as a post office in the Cherokee Nation of Indian Territory.

However, before that its post office was named Metz, which was established in 1887, and before that the place was known for a time as California Station – as to why, many historians aren't sure.

Nowata is believed to be from a Delaware Indian word, with the slightly different spelling of Noweta, which means "welcome."

But there's also a folktale about how the town got its name.

Years ago, the story goes, one day during one of the driest summers in history, a stagecoach had stopped at a road ranch of sorts in the northeast part of the territory for a change of horses and brief rest for the passengers.

A lady passenger, apparently from the East and wearing fancy attire, stepped down from the coach and was immediately appalled at the sight of some youngsters playing in the dirt, their faces covered with dust.

"Heavens!" she said. "Why doesn't someone give those poor little children a bath?"

An elderly Indian man standing nearby, his arms crossed and stoically looking straight ahead, had overheard, and offered his terse explanation:

"Can't. NOWATA!"

More than 115 years after Nowata began, not all residents were familiar with that particular story – but some of them had jokes of their own about the town's name.

Among the most popular local tales was that the town was named when a tired and thirsty traveler, who was walking from Georgia, found a local spring to be dry, so put up a sign: "No Wata."

Jeannie Inman, a Nowata County historian of nearby Delaware, repeated one to the effect of "we have 'no wata' because Stillwater stole it all."

For several years such jokes about Nowata's name had been passed around, especially during a dry summer, which residents say can be often.

Max January, a former local real estate appraiser in his early 60s who later lived in Mancos, Colorado, said he had heard so many weather anecdotes about Nowata "I get tired of hearing 'em."

But both Inman and January recalled a story that had been often told by the late Larry Jordan, an oil field "pipeliner" of nearby Lenapah:

"Back when it rained for forty days and forty nights, Nowata only got one-sixteenth of an inch."

But Marlene Kincaide, secretary of the Nowata Chamber of Commerce, said that kind of talk portrays a misleading picture of the Nowata area – although she says she's probably heard all those jokes, too.

Actually, she said, "we have the greenest Oklahoma you've ever seen – rolling hills and big, green trees. I love it!"

However, she added, "right now, we haven't had any rain for no telling how long."

Corner (circa 1889) – 'Bootlegger' and Four Nooses

Corner is believed to have begun in the late 1880s as a saloon on the bank of the Canadian River in the Pottawatomie and Shawnee lands of Indian Territory – and for the most part was never anything more than a saloon.

The site would eventually be in a remote area of Oklahoma's Pottawatomie County.

It may have been so named because of its location – in the southeastern corner of that reservation; or a place that, by at least the next year, would be the southeastern corner of the new Oklahoma Territory.

However, it's also speculated that Corner was from a corrupted version of the name of the first saloon owner, Bill Conners.

Corner is also known as the place where the term "Bootlegger" was coined — plus as the origin of a murder-for-hire plot that resulted in the lynching of four men in a livery barn in Ada.

Regardless of how the place got its name, it's believed that throughout the lifetime of Corner, a saloon was about all that was there (although a Corner post office opened on March 4, 1903, and closed three years later).

And, it's been described as the wildest, meanest, vilest, filthiest and overall most godless place in present-day Oklahoma.

It's said that victims of frequent gunfights and knifings – along with drunks killed simply for what they had in their pockets – wound up in shallow graves behind the saloon, or floating down the river.

As to its "bootlegger" reputation, legend has it that since for a time the saloon was on the border of the two territories – making it a key location for liquor sales - it was common for a cowboy to come in and buy a bottle to put in his boot, and ride off.

As a bartender once said, it was an easy way for the riders to sneak the whiskey into Indian Territory — "in their boot, down next to their leg."

Years later, three men had a discussion in the saloon about a man with whom they had a dispute, mainly over business matters. They agreed to get someone to kill him, and that Jim Miller – known as "Deacon Jim" — a notorious hired killer from Texas, was the ideal man for the job.

So, soon after the shotgun ambush slaying of rancher A.A. "Gus" Bobbitt, the three men – Joe Allen, Jesse West and Berry Burrell – plus Jim Miller, were arrested and jailed in Ada.

And soon after that, in the early morning of April 19, 1909, all four men were discovered hanged in the nearby livery barn.

It was said the lynching was performed by the local Masons. However, the case – if ever investigated - was never solved.

More than 115 years after the possible beginning of Corner, the site was mainly one of sand, tall weeds and old cottonwood trees.

But Corner had left its mark in history.

Herman Kirkwood, a native of nearby Konawa and a retired Oklahoma City police officer in his early 60s, said the Corner Saloon probably set a record for "more whiskey sold, and more people shot."

Kirkwood, also a veteran historian who headed a group called Lawmen & Outlaws in Oklahoma, said the small area that included the saloon represented the largest history of lawlessness and violence "in the whole state of Oklahoma."

The river, he said, had long washed away any trace of the old saloon, and of its nameless victims.

Loco (1890) – A Town with Savvy

Loco, in present-day Stephens County in southern Oklahoma, began on June 3, 1890, when its post office opened in the part of the present county that was then the Chickasaw Nation of Indian Territory.

It's been said the place was named for locoweed, a plant with white, yellowish or purple flowers — and from the Spanish word for "crazy," because of its undesirable effect on livestock that grazes on it.

However, it's questionable whether the name of the town has anything to do with the weed, since botanists say locoweed doesn't normally grow in that area.

Besides, it's reported that the late Ora Marsh, a longtime resident, once claimed the name is Latin from *Loco Citato* (meaning "in the place cited"), and was suggested by a physician who was one of the area's first settlers.

But regardless of where the name came from, Loco people over the years have heard plenty of jokes about it, but haven't minded being laughed at. In fact, it's made the town somewhat famous.

Margie Fondren, who for a time was the town's mayor as well as the temporary postmaster, once said the name was popular to have on

outgoing mail. She said people would come in with something to mail, "and ask us to postmark it 'Loco' – sometimes to send it to their grandkids or someone."

Around 115 years after the local post office was established, residents of the small town, amid concerns about area wildfires, still heard stories and other comments about the name – and made some of their own.

Mike Lockwood, a man in his early 50s who operated the Loco Grocery, repeated a story he heard "about a horse that ate some weeds and went crazy."

But he said remarks about Loco were like the wind that occasionally whipped the grassfires. The topic of the town's name, he said, "comes up every now and then – and then it dies down, then comes back up again."

But undoubtedly the best story about Loco was one of how a local merchant, the late Winston Campbell, proved that there was nothing crazy about his business sense.

Bob McCurry, a Loco oil field pumper in his late 70s, recalled that sometime in the 1980s, Campbell began selling caps with "Loco" on the front.

"A lot of people here laughed at 'im – they didn't think they'd sell," McCurry said. "But they showed up all over the world – all over Europe and everywhere else, I think.

"I mean, he sold a bunch of 'em!"

94 / What a Dirty Shame! 101 Unforgettable Place Names of Oklahoma

Okarche (1890) – 'Bless you!'

Okarche, pretty much in what now is central Oklahoma and on the line between Kingfisher and Canadian counties, began in 1890 in the eastern edge of the Cheyenne and Arapaho lands, by that time in Oklahoma Territory – two years before that reservation was opened to settlement. Its post office opened on June 28, 1890.

Historical records indicate that until the Cheyenne and Arapaho run in 1892, Okarche, mainly a German settlement, was little more than the post office and a cattle-loading station, and was a short distance west across the 98th meridian from the Unassigned Lands, or Old Oklahoma.

Okarche is formed by the words Oklahoma, Arapaho and Cheyenne – a name that its creator obviously thought was fitting.

However, some people have fun telling it another way:

Back when the place was first settled, the pioneer folks were having a big outdoor meal and get-together, and the man on the speaker's platform said they should name their new community, and he asked for suggestions.

Just then one of the biggest eaters – who also liked lots of pepper on his barbecue – interrupted the meeting with a thunderous, deafening, earth-jarring sneeze.

After a moment of awkward silence, the gent on the speaker's stand, feeling pressured to do something, said the first thing that came to mind:

"Well, if there are no more suggestions, I reckon 'O-KAR-CHEE!' will do just fine."

There are other versions of the story, but all have to do with a sudden loud spasmodic expiration of breath through the nose and mouth.

A little more than 115 years after the Okarche post office was established, Ann DeFrange, a reporter and columnist for *The Daily Oklahoman* newspaper who once lived in Okarche, said she often had been treated to the town's colorful legend by her grandfather, Pete

Maschino, who operated a creamery there during the 1930s and '40s.

"I think it was an Indian who sneezed," she said in describing the particular tale she heard.

And when her granddad told it, she said, "I loved the special effects – a big, loud sneeze that made all the kids squeal and giggle."

Eldorado (1890) – 'All That Glisters ...'

Eldorado, in present-day Jackson County of Oklahoma, began in 1890 when that previously discussed southwestern part of the state was still Texas. Its post office opened on Sept. 1 of that year.

Probably the only thing that makes Eldorado stand out above many small Oklahoma towns is its colorful name.

It's from the Spanish term *El Dorado,* literally meaning "the bronzed one" but commonly translated as "city of gold." Also, the term refers to a 16th century South American legend of "a place of fabulous wealth."

However, Spanish explorers likely wouldn't recognize the name if they heard it pronounced the way it is in Eldorado, Oklahoma. That's because local folks – except for a few who speak Spanish — call it "Elder-AIDA."

Around 115 years after the beginning of Eldorado, the community remained a trade center in the region of wheat, cotton and cattle, and was considered a pleasant and friendly — albeit less than booming — place to live.

Myrna Taylor, who had become a resident and Realtor in Deming, New Mexico, said she once lived in the Eldorado area — and recalled how, during her high school days, "when we were out for lunch, we would drag main – the whole three blocks."

Regarding "Eldorado," local postmaster Betty Shumaker said her post office wasn't the only one of that name in the nation. She listed nearly a dozen, with various spellings, in Arkansas, Texas, Kansas, Missouri, Colorado, California, Iowa, Illinois, Ohio and Wisconsin.

"It's a popular name, I guess," she said. "Everybody's looking for that city of gold."

And both she and David Burge, an official of the local Great Plains

National Bank, acknowledged that the town's name in Oklahoma wasn't particularly fitting.

"We're not as strong as we once were," Burge, a local resident in his middle 60s, said of the local economy. "I don't think anybody's found any gold here."

And Betty Shumaker put it this way:

"The whole downtown is just abandoned. We've sure got a few crumbling buildings."

Hope (1890) – Still Plenty of It

Hope, in Stephens County of southern Oklahoma, began as a post office on Nov. 25, 1890, in what was then the Chickasaw Nation of Indian Territory.

According to written reports, Hope was so named because town organizers expressed "local optimism for the future."

Hope is known as the home of the late Howard McCasland, noted oil business executive and onetime scholar and athlete at the University of Oklahoma at Norman, where he's honored by the Howard McCasland Field House, according to Roy "Pee Wee" Carey, director of the Stephens County Museum in Duncan.

About 115 years after Hope's beginning, it was a scattered rural community involving a church and a cemetery, and in the vicinity of Clear Creek Lake and Lake Humphreys.

And while its post office had closed in 1913, it retained its identity. The name of the place apparently still had plenty of meaning — and the place plenty of spirit.

Mark Hays, pastor of the Hope Community Church, said optimism was often the message of sermons – as well as the obvious attitude of the some 70 members of his congregation.

"The remarkable thing to me is, some eighty-seven years later, the people are still determined to continue to go on," Hays said, referring to the church that was established in 1918.

Hays, a resident of nearby Marlow in his early 40s, also worked as a field deputy for the county assessor's office in Duncan.

The community of Hope, he said, "is one of the few where residents are willing and eager to hang around."

Among those who did was Mike Waggoner, an oil field worker and heavy equipment operator in his early 50s who also saw to the upkeep of the cemetery.

He said that while the Hope name didn't attract comments every day, the community remained strong, and was a nice place to live.

And he said that while some rural residents like to drive to more populated areas to worship on Sunday, there were others like him who didn't.

"I go to church here," he said, explaining that he was different from many modern people. "A lot of people just don't understand country livin'."

Fairmount Cemetery (circa 1890) – A Good Horse

Fairmount Cemetery, now considered the official burial ground for the town of Hollis, in Harmon County in the southwest corner of Oklahoma, apparently began with a single grave sometime in 1890 in the earlier described Old Greer County region that was then Texas.

It would be 11 years before Hollis itself was settled. Its post office opened on Oct. 31, 1901 – in what by that time had become part of Oklahoma Territory.

According to the accepted story about the cemetery, one night in 1890 a lone cowboy – who was never identified – rode in and bedded down in a farmer's barn, but didn't survive until sunup. That's when he was found dead.

No one knew him, or anything about him.

However, apparently the local folks were less interested in who he was than they were in the horse he had ridden in on. It's believed that someone said, "Well, whoever he was, he was riding a fair mount."

So he was buried nearby. And finally his grave, covered with rocks, was in the southeast corner of the large, well-kept cemetery – and, after a local fund drive a century after the stranger's death, dignified with a stone bearing a nice drawing and the words, "The Fairmount Cowboy 1890."

Many in the community were moved, including local writer Jean Bartlett Brozek, who penned a poem, "The Ballad of the Fairmount Cowboy." It ended with the words:

Was he a drifter, a man with purpose,
Or an outlaw just covering ground?
Only God knows who lies in that cemetery,
Just a little southwest of town.

Some 115 years after the cowboy's death, Arlis Motley, a retired local farmer and cattleman in his early 80s, told the story behind the cemetery's name. He said it was one of his early-day ancestors, Hugh Whisenant, who gave the lone rider a place to sleep that night.

"That was my great-grandfather that put him there – he put him up in the barn," Motley said, explaining that the man "just rode in one night – this was just open country, you know – and his horse had fallen with him and hurt him. He died during the night, there in the barn."

Motley said the stranger was put away decently on an edge of his great-grandfather's place.

"That was the first grave out there," he said. "They dug it on a sand hill – it was the easiest place to dig a grave, I guess."

Motley said there was some expense to the burial, but the cowboy's horse was sold to take care of that.

And regardless of how much money the horse sold for, it was believed the new owner was proud.

Oologah (circa 1890) – 'Will'

Oologah is significant partly because of its name. Will Rogers once said "No one but an Indian can pronounce 'Oologah.'"

He likely said that before he had any idea the place would someday be remembered as his birthplace.

Oologah (pronounced "OO-la-gah"), named for Oologah (occasionally spelled Oolagah), or "Dark Cloud," a chief of the Cherokees, possibly was settled in 1890 in the Cherokee Nation of Indian Territory, its post office opening on May 25, 1891. The town would later become part of Rogers County of northeastern Oklahoma.

Will Rogers, a part-Cherokee born Nov. 4, 1879, was the wandering, outgoing young cowboy who became the rope-spinning, gum-chewing humorist who said "I never met a man I didn't like." And the whole world knew he meant it.

He went from being a virtuoso with a lariat in Wild West shows and vaudeville to being a newspaper columnist, radio commentator and author, being voted one year as the most popular male actor in Holly-

wood, and to finally being known worldwide. He's been called "the entertainer of kings and commoners."

His open way of making people laugh at themselves, especially during troubled times when they needed to, made him America's best-loved philosopher.

He was a favorite son of both his state and his country before he died in the historic plane crash in Alaska with his good friend, aviator Wiley Post, on Aug. 15, 1935.

In Oklahoma, he has continued to walk the land.

Around 115 years after Oologah's beginning, the town was centered around a life-size bronze monument called "The Cherokee Kid," a portrayal of Will, with his horse, Comanche, stopping for a drink at the old town pump.

The monument, by sculptor Sandra Van Zandt and impressionist Gary Moeller, commissioned by the Oologah Historical Society, had been unveiled about 10 years before by Will's son, Jimmy Rogers, and actor and rodeo roper Ben Johnson of Pawhuska.

Also nearby was a model of the Rogers family home; and near town was Will's birthplace, the Dog Iron Ranch, open for visitors.

The town pump monument was near the site of the old train depot, where Will met his future wife, Betty Blake – and of whom he once said "When I roped her, that was the star performance of my life."

Part of Oologah was the setting for the 1952 movie, "The Will Rogers Story," in which another son, actor Will Rogers Jr., played his father.

That movie, along with "The Story of Will Rogers," a documentary narrated by actor Bob Hope, is among many relating to Rogers' life. The films were among the collection of memorabilia and displays in the Will Rogers Memorial Museum at nearby Claremore, where Will is buried.

Oologah, as Will's hometown, was still visited regularly as it had been for a long time – but possibly more so in recent years, said Sherry Greife, president of the town's chamber of commerce.

She said much of the town had been re-done, back to its historic look, designed with Will Rogers in mind.

"It's just an absolutely gorgeous downtown area," she said, "and his personality comes out – the whole town now has that feel."

And many visitors agreed that Will probably would think so, too.

Spook Light Road (circa 1890) – 'Looking For His Head'

The Spook Light Road, near present-day tiny Peoria in Ottawa County of northeastern Oklahoma, may have become known to the general public in the early 1890s when that region was in the Peoria and Quapaw reserves in the northeastern corner of Indian Territory – and shortly before the towns of Miami and Peoria were established.

However, the legend of the "spook light" could have had its beginning before the particular road existed – as it apparently was reported occasionally, simply as "that strange light!"

For many years, it's said the light has been seen on an unpaved road leading westward from the Missouri state line, and has been described as everything from a faraway flicker to something like a blinding glare from a flying saucer.

Area resident Joe Johnson once said the light floated through the woods, causing his dogs to bark and carry on something awful.

Harold Allen, later a resident of Commerce, told of seeing it in about 1946, right over where he and some friends were in a parked car – and he called it "a big ball of light ... and you could read a newspaper by it if you wanted to!"

Others have told of the legends behind the light, including the most popular one passed along some years back by Robert Whitebird of Quapaw, former chief of the Quapaw tribe.

He said it involved an Indian couple – known for their lack of marital bliss.

"I guess he treated her bad," he said, until one night when the husband came in late and the wife ended the marriage by hitting him with an ax. It struck him just above the shoulders, and it was a mighty blow. His head rolled across the floor.

Others have explained the legend further. "And when you see that light going through the woods," one storyteller confided in earnest whispers, "it's that poor man walking along carrying a torch, looking for his head."

Some 115 years after the estimated naming of Spook Light Road, little had changed in the area of the road near Peoria, and it was still often discussed.

Harold Allen, in his late 70s, still remembered his experience on the road nearly 60 years before, and thought of it often.

And his wife, Yvonne, said he apparently wasn't the only one. "Seems like more people than ever – younger people, too – are out there looking for the Spook Light."

Could be, they had heard about the man carrying a torch.

Chickiechokie (1891) – Chickie and Reba

Chickiechokie, which eventually became Chockie, in present-day Atoka County of southeastern Oklahoma, began in 1891 in the Choctaw Nation of Indian Territory. Its post office opened on June 17 of that year.

The place is notable because of both its unusual name and its significance.

It was named for early settler Charles LeFlore's two daughters, Chickie and Chockie. Chickie later became Mrs. Lee Cruce, the second First Lady of Oklahoma. The town's name was changed to honor the second daughter in 1904.

Chockie is especially known as the home country of Reba McEntire, the singing cowgirl with an Oklahoma twang who is recognized worldwide as a star on stage, screen and television, and a country music legend.

Having grown up on a ranch and in a rodeo family, she sang the "Star Spangled Banner" at the 1975 National Finals Rodeo in Oklahoma City – and her career took off like a fast quarter horse.

After joining the Grand Ole Opry, she acted in a few movies, starred in a TV series, and then starred in Broadway's "Annie Get Your Gun" as Annie Oakley – a role that has been called one she was born to play.

Reba became the first country music performer in the hall of Great Western Performers at the National Cowboy & Western Heritage Museum in Oklahoma City – where she shares a unique honor with her father, Clark McEntire, and grandfather, John Wesley McEntire. As world calf-roping title holders, both men are in the museum's Rodeo Hall of Fame.

About 115 years after the beginning of Chickiechokie, what remained was the tiny town of Chockie, a quiet and pastoral community to the north of Atoka Lake.

And it was easy to find people familiar with the name McEntire, and Reba.

And some probably would say that if she hadn't started singing, she likely would have become well-known anyway.

That's because her first appearances in the arena were as a barrel racer – and a good one.

Grand (1892) – A Fine Mystery

Grand began in 1892 as a town in the recently opened Cheyenne and Arapaho Indian lands of Oklahoma Territory, its post office being established on Nov. 4 of that year.

The place is not only remembered for its intriguing name, but for a few mysteries, one involving a grave – apparently the only grave in the whole community.

For a time Grand was a small but active town and the seat of Day County, Oklahoma Territory, and the site eventually became the headquarters of a ranch in present-day Ellis County of western Oklahoma.

Official records say it was named for Grandville Alcorn, son of Robert Alcorn, a local judge.

However, another story about the name has it that early settlers – possibly tired and on a very warm day — used that term to describe the clear, cool water from the nearby Upper Robinson Spring.

Chapters in Grand's history describe gun battles between feuding ranchers, and courtroom antics by colorful, pistol-toting lawyer Temple Houston, son of Sam Houston.

Another is about the arson burning of the courthouse sometime in 1896 and an ensuing grand jury investigation — which failed to solve the case.

But probably the mystery that has lingered the longest involves a shooting death, without any known witnesses; and the lonely grave of the victim, whoever he was.

It's said that in the dark, early hours of a fall morning in 1896, a gunshot in the Shamrock Saloon took the life of the owner, believed to be Harry Leslie, alias William Latta.

It was never determined whether Leslie, or Latta – if either of those names was correct — was killed by someone, or by his own hand; or why he was buried by himself on a nearby rise, and the grave left unmarked for close to a century.

Grand, it seemed, never had a cemetery; it was surmised that most of the town's deceased were taken elsewhere for burial, possibly to be away from the occasional floods of the nearby Canadian River.

Anna May Lentz of Arnett, a native of Grand who for years was considered an authoritative local historian, had suggested the saloon owner was buried where he was simply as a matter of convenience.

"They did not have a cemetery as such right at Grand," she once said, speculating that, when the saloon owner was killed, "someone said 'Let's bury him over there on the slope.' And that's what they did."

Regardless of how and why it all happened, some 97 years after the Shamrock Saloon shooting, Rex Holloway, who then was the rancher at the former site of Grand, offered a short explanation:

"They just buried him on the hill all by his lonesome."

At that time, in February 1993, Holloway and two other area residents, Charles Word and Max Miller, held a brief ceremony and marked the man's grave, "Harry Leslie."

However, soon after that historians found old newspaper reports indicating Leslie was also known as William Latta.

Nearly 115 years after Grand began, the town had long vanished, its post office having closed in 1943, and the place was a quiet area in the rolling country of sagebrush and sand plums. At the site was a historical marker at the rock remnants of the former courthouse, a modest ranch home and a clear, pristine pond.

Rex Holloway was looking forward to the next Old Day County Reunion, an event held every July and a tradition believed to be more than 100 years old.

Holloway, by this time a man in his middle 80s, and others in the area, including his daughter, Connie Shoaf of nearby Arnett, usually coordinated the event – which traditionally hosted people in cars and pickups and others horseback and with wagons and teams.

The riders and teamsters were part of the annual South Canadian Trail Ride, a three-day journey up the Canadian River from Camargo. The yearly ride had been initiated in 1965 by the late Emery Fairchild of Camargo, and the upcoming ride was being coordinated by Larry White, a livestock dealer in his late 40s from Vici.

For several years the traditional ride had ended at the reunion — just in time for the tired horseman and drivers to join the people already there for the huge mid-day "dinner under the shade trees."

And, especially for the youngsters, a swim in the clear, cool pond.

Dogtown (circa 1892) – Howlin' Days of Summer

Dogtown, believed to have begun in the early 1890s in the Creek Nation of Indian Territory, eventually became a community scattered through the timber and farmland below the North Canadian River in McIntosh County of eastern Oklahoma.

The place apparently maintained an identity until the 1950s as a few farms and rural homes south of a bend of the river and east of Dustin.

For a time it was served by the Crawford School, named for local farmer Robert Wade Crawford – who, it was said, raised race horses and sold moonshine whiskey, although he didn't drink it himself.

The origin of its name – "Dogtown" and sometimes called "Dogtown Bottom," which also referred to a larger area – is unclear.

However, theories range from reports of onetime colonies of prairie dogs to even the mispronunciation of *hog,* as it's been said that packs of swine once roamed and rooted throughout the river bottom.

But more popular stories are about discussions of the region's sultry conditions during "dog days" of summer, hordes of barking "coon hounds" – and even about the local economy.

Nearly 115 years after the apparent beginning of Dogtown, the onetime community was mainly a stretch of rural land crossed by the Indian Nation Turnpike 10 miles or so south of Henryetta.

Maggie Smith of Dustin said she and husband J.J., a retired rancher in his early 80s, once farmed and rode horses to work cattle throughout the Dogtown area. And she called summers in the bottom hot and humid, and the country rugged.

"We've baled enough hay and chased enough cows down there to know. It sure gets hot," she said. "And city folks wouldn't believe anybody would ever live there."

Louise Robertson, a Dustin area resident and former postmaster there, recalled visits to a friend in what she knew as Dogtown Bottom during the 1940s.

She had memories of an "old swinging bridge" that once spanned the river – and of the local climate:

"There were so many trees and such, you couldn't get any air."

One "Dogtown" explanation was passed down from the late Hugh "Buck" Nall, an early-day resident.

Wanda Lee Crawford Schreiner of Norman, Nall's niece, said he described how "old hound dogs" at one time raised a racket that pervaded the whole community.

And Dr. Terry J. Schreiner, a dentist at Duncan who was in his late 50s, repeated in detail the story told by his great uncle:

"There was this feller that lived at the other end of the road that had all of these dogs that was always a howlin' and a squallin'."

Buck Nall had said the name was the natural result of "such a ruckus."

Still another thought came from Stoney Hardcastle of Wilburton, a retired teacher and a writer of history and folklore. He suggested the name referred to the local level of society.

"Used to," said Hardcastle, a man in his middle 80s, "people would say 'We're goin' to the dogs – goin' down to Dogtown!'"

Horsethief Canyon (circa 1892) – A Catchy Name

Horsethief Canyon, a rugged area just south of the Cimarron River in Oklahoma's present-day Payne County, may have been first called that in the early 1890s when it was in the recently opened Iowa Indian lands of Oklahoma Territory.

The canyon overflows with legends. With its thick timber and steep bluffs, rock overhangs ideal for shelter and hiding, and even the possible remains of makeshift rail fences, it has stories galore about Old West outlaws.

However, the same setting produces mental pictures of camps for line-riding cowboys, and even drifters seeking rest after wandering either horseback on afoot.

It's believed that in later years the canyon was a favorite place for law-abiding picnickers and campers, and included such Oklahoma notables as Gordon W. "Pawnee Bill" Lillie, and rodeo people representing the old 101 Ranch Wild West Show.

Definitely one of the visitors to the canyon was Frank "Pistol Pete" Eaton of nearby Perkins, the cowboy whose weathered, two-gunned, mustachioed image became the logo for Oklahoma State University as well as New Mexico State University and the University of Wyoming.

Around 115 years after the conjectured naming of Horsethief Canyon, the place still had its early-day rugged atmosphere, plus had also become known the site of a tourist attraction with the same name.

Ben Holder, a man in his late 50s, and his wife, Teresa, lived in the area, and after opening their place to the public more than 20 years before, continued to operate a center for hiking, camping and nature study, for donations.

Ben, along with state tourist officials and others, believed that, in addition to its natural scenery and legends, Horsethief Canyon attracted visitors and attention in general because of its captivating name.

And some historians believe the most memorable thing about the place involved an event that occurred there around the time of statehood:

It's said that while the irony may not have been obvious to the participants, one of the largest social gatherings in Horsethief Canyon was by the Anti-Horsethief Association.

Buzzards' Roost (circa 1892) – Jesse James?

Buzzards' Roost, a distinctive mound just outside the small town of Cement, in Caddo County of southwestern Oklahoma, may have acquired its name in the early 1890s when it was part of the Comanche, Kiowa and Apache lands of Oklahoma Territory.

If so, it's called that not simply because of its reputation as a gathering place for vultures – but because of stories of human slaughter that conjure up especially gruesome pictures.

However, the rocky, brushy knoll about 100 feet tall a short distance southeast of Cement is perhaps best known as a legendary one-time hiding place for outlaws' loot, and indeed is considered the symbol of Oklahoma's part in the saga of Jesse James.

It's been said that gold was stashed there by brothers Jesse and Frank James, the former Confederate guerrillas from Missouri who became nationally notorious bandits in the 1860s and '70s. Throughout some 15 years following the Civil War, their names were linked to brazen holdups in about a dozen states and territories.

About 115 years after the possible naming of Buzzards' Roost, the rugged hill remained a popular landmark and topic of conversation.

And local history – much of it pertaining to the mound - was portrayed through photos, printed material and relics in the Cement Museum and Jesse James Visitors' Center, a two-story building across the street from the town library.

According to a collection of reports, Buzzards' Roost may have first been called "Lone Hill," and later, alluding to stories about the James brothers, "J.J. Hill" – and still later, the name that graphically tells of warfare between white settlers and local Indians, apparently Kiowa or Comanche, or both tribes.

Monte Snider, a Cement druggist in his middle 50s and considered a foremost local historian, cited reports of "a wagon train massacre" by Indians in the 1890s in the vicinity of the mound – "where buzzards would come and perch."

And there's another story, he said:

When settlers were under attack by the Indians, they would run their horses as far up the steep mound as they could, then jump off their mounts and scramble to the top – "then shoot from the top, and one by one, pick the Indians off."

And following such a battle, he said, "the skeletons would be down below, and the buzzards would come and roost on top, and fly down and pick at the bones."

So, Snider said, while the mound probably had other names at first, "a good bet is, it changed to 'Buzzards' Roost' in the 1890s."

Other stories continued to surround Buzzards' Roost, too.

Raymond Ramos, an Oklahoma City resident in his middle 90s who had lived near Cement some 80 years earlier, said Buzzards' Roost held some of his favorite memories.

"We used to climb to the top," he said, recalling when he and a brother, Jeci, played there as youngsters. "I'll never forget Buzzards' Roost, where we used to go, just to get up there and gaze around the country."

And to longtime area resident Otto Weedn, a retired oil field worker who was nearing 80, Buzzards' Roost had even a fonder connotation.

It was atop the mound, he recalled, that he enjoyed an evening picnic and watermelon feast during a double date. That was also when he took special notice of the other boy's date, pretty Clara Sanders.

Otto said he often thinks of that evening when he passes Buzzards' Roost, and that he figured he definitely would on Sept. 19 of 2006 – his and Clara's 60th wedding anniversary.

Okeene (circa 1892) – Snakes Alive!

Okeene, in what is now Blaine County of northwestern Oklahoma, is believed to have been settled sometime in 1892 in the Cheyenne and Arapaho lands of Oklahoma Territory. Its post office was established on Jan. 27, 1893.

The name is significant because it's formed by the words Oklahoma, Cherokee and Cheyenne.

However, to many people, the name is also synonymous with snakes. The town has proclaimed itself as "Home of the World's Oldest Rattlesnake Hunt."

It's said that the hunt originated in 1939, with the late Orville VonGulker as its founder. And while there were many other annual rattlesnake hunts organized since then, especially in Oklahoma and in Texas, the Okeene hunt is believed to be the nation's first.

The annual Okeene Rattlesnake Hunt, usually held in early May, is a three-day extravaganza following the return of snake hunters from the nearby Gypsum Hills.

It often involves a parade, a snake auction and presentation of awards – one for the longest snake caught and another, the "White Fang Award," for any unfortunate person who gets bitten. There's also the honoring of a "Miss Snake Charmer."

Around 115 years after its supposed beginning, Okeene, at the crossroads of State Highways 8 and 51, was still an active community.

And the snake hunt remained the town's big annual event, said Lee Ann Barnes, director of the local library, and she added that the supply of snakes has been sufficient every year:

"We still have plenty of those things."

The Okeene hunt also apparently remained popular with rattlesnake enthusiasts in other parts of the state and nation.

At least one longtime snake hunter, John Sigle of Oklahoma City, said the snake extravaganza at Okeene, in terms of people turnout and the number and size of snakes, was one of the best.

"There are thousands of people there, and a lot of snakes," said Sigle, a cardiac nurse in his late 40s who had hunted the reptiles for several years. "And no doubt about it, they've got some big rattlers there."

Paul Johannesmeyer, a 50-year-old local farmer who had long been familiar with the snake hunt, mentioned that the event started after some large rattlesnakes were brought into town after being shot – "and I guess a hundred people showed up to see those dead snakes."

He said Orville VonGulker, a local newsman, then said "If that many people like to see dead snakes, I wonder how many would come here to see 'em alive."

And many people did come, and have continued to virtually every year.

Maria Nease, a local insurance agent, agreed that the hunt had become a big local attraction – even if she personally wasn't very enthusiastic about it.

She said she was "one of those few residents that tend to leave town on that weekend."

Saddle Mountain (circa 1893) – The Peak of Nostalgia

Saddle Mountain, a rocky landmark that juts out of the rolling plains at the edge of the Wichita Mountains, may have been so named in the early 1890s when that area was in the Comanche, Kiowa and Apache lands of Oklahoma Territory.

It's speculated it was first called that by non-Indians who were in the reservation in the 1890s – some eight years before that region was officially opened to settlement in 1901.

It also was the designation of the Saddle Mountain Indian Mission that was near there for a time, plus became the name of a nearby town in about 1901. Its post office opened on Jan. 22 of the next year.

The Saddle Mountain community finally dwindled to a vacated cobblestone store building in what had become Kiowa County in southwestern Oklahoma, the structure serving as a volunteer fire department headquarters and a museum.

For several years the unofficial curator of the little house of history was Margaret O'Pry who lived nearby. She and her husband, Carl, had once operated the store that was built in the 1920s. The first store building at the site was reportedly owned by Harry Swinford and Sam McMichael.

Legends that clung to the peak over the years involved Indian beliefs that the "medicine mountain" had curing powers, and stories that outlaws had stashed gold there, "under a rock with a turkey track on it."

Names symbolic of that region that were depicted in the museum included those of such noted Kiowas as onetime Chief Santana (also spelled Santanta), or White Bear, and Tsa-Toke, or Hunting Horse, said to have been an Army scout during frontier days; Melvin Askew, a calf roper who was killed as a soldier in World War II; and John Taylor, another local cowboy who became the first president of the Oklahoma Farm Bureau.

Especially featured with photos and write-ups was Delf A. "Jelly" Bryce, the once nationally famous lawman and quick-draw artist. A native of nearby Mountain View, as a youngster he reportedly had spent time – particularly when target practicing — in the Saddle Mountain area.

Nearly 115 years after the supposed naming of Saddle Mountain, the cobblestone building remained, still as a museum, but open by appointment only. The local post office had closed in 1955.

Nearby was the Indian Mission Cemetery, with tombstones of such notables as missionary Isabel Crawford and Rev. Lucius Aitson, her Kiowa interpreter.

And Saddle Mountain itself still held its charm, at least for nearby residents.

Bill Sims, a farmer and rancher and native of the area in his late 60s, called the land formation "the focal point of the community."

"There's something about that peak," he said. Even with other mountains in the vicinity and if you were some 15 miles away, he said, "when you get over in one direction and look over the horizon, that mountain stands out alone.

"For some reason, when you look that way, that's the mountain you see."

Dessie Evatt, also a native of the community – and who once clerked in the local store during the 1940s — said she still enjoyed the view, usually every evening.

"At night is the best time," she said. "I sit on the porch and look over that way. It's pretty — all of it."

Lost City (circa 1893) – Found by a Star

Lost City is remembered both because of its intriguing name and the fact it has the reputation of being the only place in Oklahoma that was actually put on the official state map by "a falling star."

The tiny community, in present-day Cherokee County of eastern Oklahoma, is believed to have begun, and gained its name, in the early 1890s in the Cherokee Nation of Indian Territory.

It's said that shortly after the community began as a coal-mining center, residents expected an economic boom – which failed to happen. So people left their tents and shacks overnight, and the place was called "lost."

There also are other stories about the origin of the name – but the true incident about the falling star surely will go down in history as the best story about Lost City.

Until one Saturday evening, Jan. 3, 1970, Lost City was virtually unknown a few miles outside of its immediate area. But on that date, at 8:14 p.m., a chunk from high above the earth plunged into a nearly snow-covered road.

It was reported that area residents heard "a scream," "a buzzing," and "a long roar," and that some who were outside saw "a flash that lit up everything."

The meteorite – the name for a meteoroid from space after it lands on earth – was discovered a few days later by the local school principal, Barney Mitchell, when he was on his way to feed his cattle.

Mitchell, who was accompanied by friend and neighbor Bill Jones, later described it as something about the size of a football that "looked like a big flint rock."

He later recalled saying to Jones: "What's that, a rock? Probably somebody's had to stop and fix a flat, and picked it up out of the ditch."

But people elsewhere were also aware that something had streaked across the sky. And the object in the road would soon appear more than that to scientists.

It drew worldwide attention as the famous "Lost City Meteorite." It was said it had come from out beyond Mars, and was "of intense scientific interest," and expected to provide valuable information toward solving the mysteries of the universe.

It also was said that, because of factors involving the meteoroid's orbit and the earth's orbit around the sun, the object's landing where it did was the result of a "trillion-to-one" chance.

Within days, virtually the whole world had heard of Lost City, Oklahoma.

And the year after that, Lost City was placed on the official state map.

Close to 115 years after the possible beginning of Lost City, the place still existed mainly as the small Lost City School, a cemetery and few homes near the clear stream of Fourteen Mile Creek.

Some area residents still recalled the discovery of the 1970 "falling star." Among them were Bill Jones, a farmer in his late 60s, and his wife, Nancy.

Bill vividly remembered the day he and Barney Mitchell saw the "flint rock" in the road, and Nancy recalled seeing the flash in the sky a few nights earlier.

And occasionally, stories were repeated about Lost City's name.

Besides the generally accepted account involving the coal-mining era, there was one about some Plains Indians, from the western part of the present state, in Oklahoma Territory, who in about 1900 had come to work in the mines.

The legend has it that they set up tepees along the creek – but after a time, because of either a hard winter or an outbreak of a serious disease, "they just left overnight."

Another story – one usually told with a grin – was that the community got its name simply "because it was so far back in the hills, you had to be lost to find it."

And regardless of the stories, Lost City remained on the map.

Geronimo (1894) – A Warrior

Geronimo, a present-day town just south of Fort Sill in Comanche County of southwestern Oklahoma, is remembered for its name — which to many historians is the one most associated with American Indians and the Western frontier, and indeed is the inspiration behind the town.

The town of Geronimo was settled in the Comanche, Kiowa and Apache lands of Oklahoma Territory not long after the reservation was opened to settlement by lottery in 1901. Its post office was established March 5, 1903.

However, the town's name goes back earlier, as it honors the famous Apache warrior, who in 1894 – more than three decades after he launched a nearly relentless war against both Mexico and the United States — was brought as a prisoner to Fort Sill, then a U.S. frontier outpost in Oklahoma Territory.

Geronimo, born either in present-day Arizona or New Mexico, waged virtually a constant battle against non-Indian authorities and settlers after his wife and children were killed by Mexican troops in 1858.

After some 28 years of fighting, and leading what has been called "the last major force of independent Indian warriors" that refused to yield to the U.S. government in the American West, he surrendered in 1886.

During his some 15 years as a prisoner at Fort Sill, he was allowed to take part in several special events throughout the nation — among them the 1905 inaugural parade for President Teddy Roosevelt.

By the time he died at Fort Sill in 1909, at the approximate age of 80, Geronimo had become one of the most bizarre celebrities in history.

Although the story of Geronimo is controversial as well as remarkable, his name evoking images of bloody atrocities and feelings ranging from sheer hatred to rapt admiration for an underdog hero, he remains an American icon, and a legend.

Towana Spivey, who for several years was director of Fort Sill's National Historic Landmark and Museum, once said of the man:

"You can't help but respect Geronimo. He fought for what he believed in."

Tim Poteete, who for a long time was a historian at the Museum of the Great Plains in Lawton, said he had often heard Geronimo called "the most famous Indian in the whole wide world."

The town of Geronimo is also remembered as the site of what has been called "the bloodiest bank robbery in Oklahoma history" – the Dec. 14, 1984, holdup and shooting deaths of four people. It resulted in the conviction of two young men, Jay Wesley Neill, who was executed, and Robert Grady Johnson, who was sent to prison for life.

More than 110 years after Geronimo, the warrior, was brought to present-day Oklahoma, his namesake town was a place of about 950 people – and where the man wasn't at all forgotten.

The town was anticipating its annual Geronimo Birthday Celebration, usually held every September. And both postmaster Wendi Ratliff and town clerk Cyndy Gregory mentioned a local belief that Geronimo himself was once there – when he and his captors stopped on their way to his future prison.

Ratliff said that according to the legend, "this is the area where they camped before they took him into Fort Sill."

Folks in Geronimo, she said, were proud of that story.

Moscow Flats (1894) – Pure Americana

Moscow Flats, in present-day Woodward County of northwestern Oklahoma, is a vernacularism for the proper name of Moscow, which was settled in the Cherokee Strip, at that time part of Oklahoma Territory and a year after the strip was opened to settlement. Moscow's post office opened on May 3, 1894.

It's believed the place was never much more than the hub of a friendly and folksy community in the farm country near the North Canadian River – and an unlikely setting for such a name.

While it's been speculated the first local storekeeper came from Russia, the origin of "Moscow" has long been a mystery.

More than 110 years after its beginning, Moscow Flats was comprised of a vacated school building, a cemetery and some homes here and there in the vicinity of the river and the highways of State Highway 50 and U.S. Highway 183. The post office had closed in 1906.

But the community still had a strong identity, and was considered the home of some pioneer families, including that of Terry Peach, who was Oklahoma's commissioner of agriculture.

In fact, when he wasn't busy at his office of the Department of Agriculture in Oklahoma City, Peach, a man in his middle 50s, was still at home in the Moscow Flats area.

And like most people from there, he said he's heard the same question over and over: "Are you all from Russia?"

"And I've always wondered, how *did* it get its name?" he said. "I hope someday to discover an answer to that."

Eldon Cox, a farmer and rancher in his early 60s – and the grandson of early-day local postmaster Lizzie Cox – had an explanation for at least part of the name of Moscow Flats.

"It *is* kind of a flat area here when you look back from the river," he said. "So everybody knows where that comes from."

Violet Springs (circa 1894) – No Flowers

Violet Springs, in the region that would finally become Pottawatomie County, Oklahoma, is remembered as a place with a pretty name that belies an ugly past.

It may have been settled in the early or middle 1890s in what was designated as B County of Oklahoma Territory.

Its post office, as Violet, opened on April 6, 1899, in the former Pottawatomie and Shawnee lands of Indian Territory. But it's believed the community, as Violet Springs, had already existed for a time.

It's reported that it was named for some nearby springs. But if so, it's apparently a mystery as to exactly when, and especially why, the name came about.

However, regardless of the origin of the name, because of the rough reputation of the place, "Violet Springs," has become known as a paradox.

Like Keokuk Falls and Corner, it was a wild "saloon town" — a hub for running whiskey to the Indians and a vile den of horse thieves, men wanted for murder, the most ferocious of cutthroats, and bad hombres in general. It was a hangout for lowlifes of the lowest kind.

It was said that among the many killings there was that of A.J. Morrison, a saloon owner who was considered the town's founder.

Violet Springs was also linked with possibly the most sickening act of vigilantism in the nation's history: the 1898 burning death of two young Seminole men in a nearby settlement.

Lincoln McGeisey and Palmer Sampson, suspected in the killing of a white woman, were seized by a mob, some of whom were from Violet Springs, and chained to a blackjack tree and set afire.

More than 110 years after the apparent settlement of Violent Springs, the community, the site of which was west of Konawa along

State Highway 39, was long gone (its post office had closed in 1906). The only reminder of the place was its cemetery.

Mickey Johnson, a longtime resident of the area, said there was no sign at all of the old community – or even of a water source that reportedly inspired the name.

"We've walked every bit of it, bird huntin' and stuff, and we've never found any place that we figured was a spring," said Johnson, a stockman and public utility firm employee in his late 40s.

But he considered the cemetery, which has been said to contain many unmarked graves, including those of the losers of gun and knife fights, sufficient to tell the story of old Violet Springs.

Kansas (circa 1894) – The Little One

Kansas, in present-day Delaware County of northeastern Oklahoma, apparently had its beginning in the early or middle 1890s in the Cherokee Nation of Indian Territory. Its post office opened on Jan. 5, 1895.

It could be no one knows for sure how the place got its name, but one story has it that one of the early visitors to the new settlement was a salesman from Kansas City – either Kansas City, Kansas, or Kansas City, Missouri.

That story was once repeated by Edith Warder, a clerk in the local J.O. Jones General Store.

The way she explained it, "a salesman from Kansas City – back then they called 'em 'peddlers' – he came in here before the place had any kind of name. And later on he was referred to as 'the man from Kansas.'"

If, in fact, it happened that way, Kansas was then adopted as the post office name.

And, apparently to avoid confusing the name of the town with that of the state, people began putting "Little" in front of it.

However, it's said that many local residents weren't fond of hearing that name, even if Kansas *was* small.

Warder had said that occasionally even some letters were addressed with "Little" before the town's name.

"But we don't like it," she said. "We say 'Kansas.'"

Kansas is said to be the home of the "Marlboro Man" – or one of them.

Darrell Winfield, who for several years was the horse wrangler depicted in national television commercials for a brand of cigarettes, reportedly was born in the Kansas area. He later lived in Wyoming, where he raised horses, and was one of the models for the Marlboro commercials.

More than 110 years after the town's beginning, Kansas remained a place with a tiny downtown area, where an old well had long been a familiar landmark. The J.O. Jones store building was still there, but the business had closed.

Vince Wright, a retired military man in his early 60s who lived in the nearby Flint Ridge resort area, called Kansas quaint but very small. "There's not much there," he said, "and it's different — right on the main street is that old well."

Local postmaster Stacey Pirsch said the name "Little Kansas" apparently had been lost in the past. "I don't hear many people saying that anymore," she said.

And folks in Kansas apparently liked it that way.

Mustang (circa 1894) – Horses and High Class

Mustang, in what finally became a Canadian County town in central Oklahoma, traces its beginning to the middle 1890s as a settlement north of the Canadian River in Oklahoma Territory. Its post office opened on Feb. 4, 1895.

However, the name itself goes back further, as records say the town was christened from nearby Mustang Creek. Exactly when that was named is hard to say.

But regardless of when the name came about, local historians feel confident that it was inspired by wild horses that roamed the grasslands in the vicinity of the stream.

(It's believed that the mention in early records of another "Mustang Creek" as a stop on a branch of the old California Road, some 60 miles to the southeast in the former Chickasaw Nation of Indian Territory, is coincidental.)

Throughout Mustang's history as a town, it's had the character of a small, rural-type community that in the 1920s was nearly wiped out by a tornado — but was rebuilt and began gaining population.

More than 110 years after the beginning of Mustang, the town, reportedly with more than 15,000 people, was considered a growing suburban center in the Oklahoma City metropolitan area.

Signs of progress were omnipresent, and included a modernistic Mustang Town Center that housed the public library and other commu-

nity offerings; and an exemplary school system. The town was becoming the center of homes and acreages that bespoke of affluence and the well-to-do.

Both Desiree Webber, director of the library, and Becky Julian, head of the chamber of commerce, said residents seemed far more interested in the present than in the town's history or its colorful name.

So did two members of the local historical society, Kenneth Bales and Glen Muse.

Bales, a 70-year-old local farmer and stockman, told of rainy seasons years ago when the Canadian would go on roaring rampages.

But during normal times, he said, there was an unusual place of business right in the middle of river — "where you could go and get liquor."

Glen Muse, a retired Federal Aviation Administration employee in his early 70s, suggested that when the devastating tornado, in about 1927, went through, "a lot of history went with it."

And as to local feelings about tradition, he said most residents "are people who came from somewhere else – and most of 'em just don't give a big hoot about the name."

However, pride in the town's name was still evident. The schools' athletic teams were the "Broncos." And there were other names like "Wild Horse Park" and various images of mustangs here and there.

The community had plenty of horses, too – though many were sleek equines definitely not of the wild type. There were places like "Thoroughbred Acres" and "Polo Estates."

And Kenneth Bales added that "I've got horses all over the place." But he said he didn't ride them as often as he once did:

"I have cattle, too, and I used to use horses a lot. But now, I just feed 'em and look at 'em, and remember the old days."

Also, Mustang was planning its 30th annual Western Days, scheduled for September.

Coeta Morrell, a charter member of the Mustang Roundup Club, said she and the rest of the some 60 members were looking forward to saddling up for the parade.

And Coeta was at least one resident who was proud of the town's name.

"About everybody who has something to do with roundup clubs and horses are familiar with Mustang," she said, adding that plenty of local people were fond of horses:

"I go out and kiss mine every morning."

Sulphur (1895) – Name with a Smell

Sulphur, in what would become Murray County of southern Oklahoma, began in 1895 in the Chickasaw Nation of Indian Territory. Its post office opened on Oct. 2 of that year.

It apparently was named from a nearby spring, with the water believed to have "medicinal" value, and which contained minerals that smell of sulfur (also spelled sulphur).

The spring, which feeds Rock Creek, at one time attracted thousands of tourists, according to records. People came by both wagon and team and train to drink the water and bathe in the creek, and even smear themselves with its mud, historians say.

Sulphur is also believed to be the only town in Oklahoma to have had a feud that was settled when the two sides literally "buried the hatchet."

The disagreement — over whether the main part of town should be east or west of the creek — ended in about 1909 with a good-natured ceremony in which a hatchet was set in the cement of a bridge over the creek.

And nearly 40 years later the hatchet was removed and taken to the chamber of commerce office, to be viewed as a symbol of local cooperation and friendship.

Around 110 years after Sulphur's beginning, the town, in the vicinity of the Arbuckle Mountains, billed itself as "The City of Springs" and the home of the Chickasaw National Recreation Area.

At the chamber of commerce – where the famous hatchet was still on display — office administrator Neita Lapine listed attractions of Sulphur, where for many years visitors had been enchanted by the town's fountain that bubbled water into an aquamarine pool, and the falls at the nearby national park.

And she said many local residents considered the water healthful. "There are still Sulphurites – people who have lived here all their lives – who go to the falls and fill their jugs every Saturday."

However, she acknowledged that not everyone liked the water for its fragrance.

"On certain days it's worse than others," she said, adding that once her grandson – William Beers, then about five years old — said the water "smelled like boiled eggs – but he probably meant rotten eggs."

Maud and Bowlegs (1896 and 1927) – Not Very Nice

Maud, slightly southeast from the center of present-day Oklahoma and in Seminole County, apparently was settled in the middle 1890s in the Seminole Nation of Indian Territory, its post office opening on April 16, 1896.

It's believed it was named for Maud Stearns, a rural mail carrier.

Bowlegs, also in Seminole County, is 10 miles or so east of Maud. Bowlegs' post office opened on April 23, 1927.

It was named for Billy Bowlegs, onetime Seminole chief.

The two towns are also the butt of a regional joke of the off-color variety – oftentimes told with a wink and by some male jester when in the company of other males.

Since a westbound traveler on State Highway 59 who is going to one town will find it on the other side of the other town, the double entendre has it that "you can't get to Maud without going through Bowlegs."

Some 110 years after Maud began, and close to 80 years after the town of Bowlegs came into being, it was hard to say when the joke about the two towns got started, but it was still being told.

Jim Jones, a retired educator of Maud who was in his late 70s, said he first heard the story when he was in high school, "and it goes around all the time."

However, Kelley Buchanan, who was director of the Maud Housing Authority, said she doubted "if the younger generation ever heard of that."

In Bowlegs, relief postmaster Dee Lewis, who grew up in another part of the state, was one person who hadn't – but obviously enjoyed hearing it for the first time.

"Oh, that's funny!" she said. "I've never heard it, but that's good – it's cute!"

Roger Copeland, a former Maud resident in his early 60s, said he once made the Maud-and-Bowlegs story nationally famous.

Copeland, a resident of Fort Worth, Texas, and the manager of a video rental store in nearby Burleson, said in the late 1960s he was interviewed on a television game show in New York. He was an Army soldier stationed in that area.

He said when he told the show's host he was from Maud, Oklahoma, and the host asked him what larger town it was near, "I said it was eleven miles from Bowlegs."

Copeland said the show host laughed — "and the whole audience did, too. They all laughed."

He also said he won a color TV set on the show.

And even though he had to score on some little games to win it, he said he felt like the judges were influenced by the fun over "Maud and Bowlegs."

Berlin (circa 1896) – Luck of the Draw

Berlin, in present-day Roger Mills County of western Oklahoma, apparently began in the middle 1890s in what had been the Cheyenne and Arapaho lands before being designated as County F of Oklahoma Territory. Its post office opened on Sept. 2, 1896.

The tiny community is remembered because of its name – from the city in Germany, but locally pronounced "BUR-len" – and because it supposedly was dubbed when names were drawn from a hat.

Major events in Berlin's history included a robbery of a local store in about 1905, during which the bandits shot and wounded the merchant and fled on horseback.

Some 110 years after it began, Berlin remained as a small but neat village a dozen miles or so south of Cheyenne and east of U.S. Highway 283.

Its post office had closed in about 1967, but it had a church, a granite historical marker, a fire station, a rodeo arena and a community center.

K.D. "Chubb" Campbell, a former local merchant and area native in his late 70s, said it was believed the perpetrators of the holdup outran a posse to Doxey, some eight miles away, left their horses and escaped by train.

He said the merchant, Tom Crawford, survived after residents administered some in-the-rough first aid – pulling a handkerchief through the wound "to wipe out the gun powder."

"The bullet had gone clear through," Campbell said. "I don't know where he was shot at."

Campbell, whose wife, Nelona, once was acting Berlin postmaster, said he was born one mile west of Berlin, "and I've still got the check my dad wrote to pay the doctor." He noted the amount was $25 — "I wasn't worth much back then."

But Chubb's favorite story was about the name Berlin. He said the area's first settlers, most of them from Missouri, were discussing what to call their community when they agreed to draw from several suggested names in a hat.

"And this German fella, who farmed out here someplace, he put the name of Berlin in," he said, "and that's what got pulled out."

However, Chubb added, the others didn't pronounce the name correctly. "They cut it short."

As to why, he wasn't sure. "They may have put that Missouri brogue on it."

Wildcat (1897) – More Like a Kitten?

Wildcat was settled in the late 1890s in the Creek Nation of Indian Territory in a site that would finally be part of present-day Okmulgee County of eastern Oklahoma.

It's remembered – though barely – because of its name, plus as a small community that apparently outgrew its onetime somewhat rough reputation.

Wildcat's post office opened on May 19 of 1897, but in 1902 changed to Grayson. And that one closed in 1929.

However, the community would linger for years, and continued to be called Grayson by many residents.

While the origin of the original name is apparently unknown, "Wildcat" has inspired many colorful theories – perhaps partly for that very reason; since regardless of the stories told – no matter how much they stained the community's image – it would be difficult to prove them false.

Over the years, some residents at a nearby place called Wildcat Junction had said Wildcat began as a center for moonshine whiskey and other illegal goings on. They said people there "used to fight like wildcats."

And a waitress in a café in that area said "people used to call it 'Cat' – you can use your imagination."

Pete Burney, a native of nearby Hoffman, once said that that region was where "every other house sold wildcat whiskey."

Burney told of one home in particular that provided both illegal spirits and live entertainment. He said customers, while consuming the liquid goods along with homemade gumbo, provided by the woman of the house, could sit and watch her husband tap-dance.

"And, boy, he could really tap-dance – especially after he had a drink or two."

Nearly 110 years after the beginning of Wildcat, the place was still there, but as the small, quiet community better known as Grayson.

And a mile or so away at Hoffman, Pete Burney, by this time a retired carpet layer in his late 60s, said he and his wife, Ruby, were hosts every Saturday night to an event he called "an old gospel singin' – some place for these old people to go."

He said the nearby small patch of homes generally known as Grayson had become "a real good place, with a community center and all, and fixed up real nice."

But he said he hadn't forgotten the days when the area was a place of "dancin' and drinkin' and fightin', and it had a lot of drunks – and I was one of 'em."

That was when, he said, the nearby community had a totally different personality – "and it's different now."

And, anymore, he said, "most people call it Grayson. But I still call it Wildcat."

Frogville (1897) – River Serenades

Frogville began in 1897 as a settlement a little north of the Red River in the Choctaw Nation of Indian Territory in what would become Choctaw County of southeastern Oklahoma. Its post office opened Oct. 29 of that year.

It's been written that the place was named because of the region's "great plethora of frogs." Stories have it that bullfrogs on the river were so large they "ate young ducks" – and at night carried on so much that people couldn't sleep.

Residents over the years have described Frogville as being in the middle of good farming country, plus near the legendary loud frogs on the river. Charles Frost once said the frogs were quite large — "and at night, they'd really talk to ya."

Longtime resident Omie Johnson once told about a bustling community with a cotton gin and "a three-teacher school."

And the frogs, she said, were "right across from the post office. And late in the evening, all over this country folks could hear those frogs hollerin.'"

Close to 110 years after the beginning of Frogville, it remained a rural area of scattered homes amid pastures and cropland and some timber. The post office had closed in 1933, but it was still on the official state map.

Larry Johnson, a farmer in his late 40s, was among the few area residents.

He said the place hadn't changed much since his ancestors lived there – except that frogs weren't heard as much as they once were, possibly because of dry weather during the past few years.

"There used to be lots of bullfrogs," he said. "There are still some, but nothing like there used to be."

Either that, or maybe modern bullfrogs are quieter.

Wildman (1900) – Mining Mayhem

Wildman is remembered as a symbol of Oklahoma's mining days, and for a name that coincidentally described its character.

Named for mining developer Frank Wildman, it began in 1900 in the Comanche, Kiowa and Apache lands of Oklahoma Territory – in present-day Kiowa County — when the federal government opened the Wichita Mountains region to mineral exploration. Its post office opened on May 3 the next year.

At first there were high hopes of what someone called "the last great gold rush east of the Rockies." One of the impressive structures was the Gold Bells Mine. And the town exploded into a population of some 500 people.

However, mainly what was mined there during its some five years was a bad reputation.

Along with fighting between landowners and miners, drinking, gambling and shootings went on day and night.

The post office, which was a structure on wheels that could be moved around like a cook shack, was said to contain a dozen bullet holes.

Meanwhile, despite some evidence of gold, silver and other minerals, the hard granite was virtually impossible to smelt.

The town's post office closed in 1904, and by statehood the mining operation, along with the town, was about gone.

More than 105 years after Wildman began, virtually all that remained of the old mine and community, south of Roosevelt and in the vicinity of Tom Steed Lake, were a few old foundations.

Pat Moore, a farmer in his middle 70s who lived in Roosevelt, said much of the area of the old mine was "just pastureland, on the edge of a mountain."

But he recalled stories from an older resident who used to travel with horse and buggy past the mine, "back when it was going full-speed – and it was mostly saloons, and where everybody carried a pistol on their hip. It was rough."

Alva "Dobber" Cook, a Roosevelt wheat harvester in his early 80s, said the old Wildman schoolhouse was hauled off to be used as a church in another community; and the cemetery had been obliterated. "The fence was torn down, and somebody plowed it up and ran over it."

And Wildman was no longer, he said. "That was the last of it."

Big Pasture (circa 1900) – Texas Cattle and Wolves

Big Pasture was a large block of land that the U.S. government, in a plan designed to benefit the Indians, set aside for cattle grazing in the Comanche, Kiowa and Apache lands of Oklahoma Territory, in what later became part of southwestern Oklahoma.

While it's hard to say when the term Big Pasture was coined – and whether by government officials, white ranchers or Indians – historical reports show it was entrenched into the English language well before 1906, which was when the reserved tract was broken up.

The land, of about 480,000 acres, was designated as the special grassland in 1900. In 1901 the Comanche, Kiowa and Apache lands, along with the adjoining Wichita and Caddo reservation, was opened to settlement; and the region known as Big Pasture was sold by sealed bids five years later.

More specifically, "the big pasture" was often applied to some

400,000 acres, the largest of several tracts of the land involved. However, the story of Big Pasture goes back further.

Historians say ranchers from nearby Texas had already been grazing their cattle in that area for several years during the 1800s, and at some point made lease arrangements with the tribes.

Cattlemen from south of the Red River continued to use the land until the reserve program ended, and probably benefited more from it than the Indians. Names of such cattle barons as Burk Burnett and the Waggoner Ranch are prominent in Big Pasture history.

The Big Pasture area is also the home of Jack "Catch 'em Alive" Abernathy, a cowboy and lawman known for capturing wolves and coyotes barehanded by jumping off on them from his running horse; and where President Teddy Roosevelt joined him for a wolf hunt in 1905.

It was said that the hunting party – which also included the respected Quanah Parker of the Comanches – bagged nearly 20 animals, after which Roosevelt thanked his hosts for "a bully good time."

Also, five years later, it was from the Big Pasture area that Jack Abernathy's two young sons, Bud and Temple, both under 12 years old, made a 2,000-mile horseback ride to Washington, D.C., and then to New York.

Abernathy's fame as a horseback wolf hunter also is believed to have inspired a bit of dialogue by actor Lee Marvin — in an indirect reference to Abernathy and the way he would "wrestle" wolves — in the Western movie "Monte Walsh," from the book by Jack Schaefer.

More than 105 years after the surmised naming of Big Pasture, its overall region covered parts of Tillman and Cotton counties, encompassing the small towns of Grandfield, Randlett, Loveland and Devol, and much ranch and farmland. The whole area had an estimated 1,800 residents.

At Grandfield, considered the center of the former Big Pasture, was a historical monument describing the significance of Big Pasture as "the last big land opening in Oklahoma."

Grandfield was also served by the weekly newspaper *Big Pasture News*. And Randlett was the location of the Big Pasture School.

Wayne Spradlin, a 70-year-old retired Civil Service worker at Grandfield who served on the local Historical Preservation Committee, suggested that the name Big Pasture may have come from a comment by rancher Burnett:

"Someone once asked him, 'Where are your cattle at?' And he said, 'Over there in the *big pasture.*'"

But Louise Michael Watson, a Grandfield retired teacher and author of a book, "Come Tour with Me – Tales of the Big Pasture," theorized that the Indians named the Big Pasture – possibly in the English language, or maybe in Kiowa, Comanche or Apache.

H. Grant Kinzer, a Grandfield native in his late 60s who was living in Las Cruces, New Mexico, where he was an agriculture professor at New Mexico State University, called the former Big Pasture "pretty rough ol' country."

He said it was an area where "you had to work like hell to make a living" – but that "I guess I think it was a pretty good place to grow up."

Another former resident of the Big Pasture area was Tom Kemp, who in his early 60s was living in the Seattle, Washington, area where he was an economist with the U.S. Department of Labor.

He said he was born "across the river in Texas," but grew up on the Oklahoma side and attended the Big Pasture School until he graduated in 1959.

And he recalled his former home country as "just flat as a table, with very few trees. You can see forever."

Dr. Bob Wyatt, a native of Grandfield who in his middle 60s was a history teacher at East Central University at Ada, recalled an incident more than 20 years earlier that gave the Big Pasture big publicity on the west coast.

Wyatt, a former editor of the Grandfield newspaper, said that in 1984 he and his son, Bobby, went to the Democratic Convention in San Francisco, California, to cover the event.

He said the name Big Pasture earned them "a full-page article" in *The San Francisco Examiner* newspaper – "about the Grandfield newspaper being the smallest newspaper in the U.S. covering the convention."

He added that the story, "though something good for us, also kind of made fun of us for the name of the paper and our provincial, small-town ideas about how a convention should be run."

He recalled one comment he heard in San Francisco to the effect of "Just what you'd expect from someone from a place called 'Big Pasture'!"

Gotebo (circa 1900) – A Popular Guy

Gotebo, a small town in present-day Kiowa County of southwestern Oklahoma, apparently began in late 1900 as a railroad stop in the Comanche, Kiowa and Apache lands of Oklahoma Territory, shortly before that area was opened to settlement the next year.

Although Gotebo's post office didn't open until Feb. 25, 1904 – following the closing of the post office at the adjoining town site of Harrison – historians say Gotebo had earlier been the name of a station on the Chicago, Rock Island and Pacific Railroad. It's believed the tracks were then being laid westward from nearby Mountain View, probably before 1901.

The town was named for Gotebo, a sub chief of the Kiowas, who died in 1927 at about age 80.

Events in Gotebo's history included a cloud burst and flood in 1903 that nearly wiped out the entire town, causing at least two deaths.

However, it was said that Gotebo himself became a hero when he saved some young children by swimming through swift currents and pulling them to safety.

But if the town of Gotebo will be remembered for anything, chances are it'll be for its intriguing name.

In Kiowa, Gotebo is said to mean "Hat Made of Ermine Pelt," and indeed carries a serious connotation – except to non-Indians.

When local folks tell someone they're from Gotebo, a typical comment is "You gotta be kiddin'!"

Or, "You mean there really *is* a place called 'Gotebo'?"

At least 105 years after its apparent beginning, tiny Gotebo was an incongruity of a ghost-town business district and nearby pretty town park next to a new-looking rodeo arena that was still in the making.

And townspeople were looking forward to their next annual celebration, the Gotebo Get Down, that's typically held every September.

As in its past celebrations, the scheduled activities were to include the telling of funny "Gotebo" stories.

Like one that had been told a few times by Leon "Red" Law, a local retired packing plant manager in his late 70s.

When he was a soldier in the Korean War many years ago, a telephone operator wouldn't believe the town's name when he tried to call home from overseas.

"Is that really a town?" she said. "Are you putting me on?"

And his Army buddies didn't remember his name, so just called him "Gotebo."

Marilyn Thurman, who has been editor of the local *Gotebo News* as well as coordinator of the celebration, said the usual storytelling and swapping of "Gotebo" jokes during the festival never offends anyone.

She said it's like "the term 'Okie' – you know, it's all right for us to say it."

Frieda Jo Ann Adams, another longtime Gotebo resident who was the postmaster for several years, said when she attended meetings in places like Washington, D.C., "I heard all kinds of comments, like 'I thought Gotebo was just a joke!'"

"I've never been anywhere," she said, "that 'Gotebo' didn't get attention. And the jokes go on, and on, and on."

She said another comment she's often heard is "Do they really rope goats in Gotebo?"

"And it so happens they do," she said. "We've had a roundup club here for many years, and they like to practice by roping goats.

"And right now every vacant lot has goats on it."

Nofire Hollow (circa 1900) – Wes Lived There

Nofire Hollow, a rural community in the hills of present-day eastern Oklahoma and on the line of Adair and Cherokee counties, may have first been called that in the early 1900s when it was in the Cherokee Nation of Indian Territory.

It apparently was so named from the Nofire family, who were early-day residents.

Nofire Hollow is known as the home of actor Wes Studi, a full-blood Cherokee who became famous as a Hollywood and television actor.

Before leaving his home country, he worked for the Cherokee Nation at its headquarters near Tahlequah. He also was a writer and columnist for the tribe's newspaper, then called *The Cherokee Advocate*.

After getting into acting, he became renowned for his roles in such movies as "The Last of the Mohicans," "Geronimo: An American Legend," "Dances with Wolves" and "Crazy Horse," and as a detective in TV productions of some of Tony Hillerman's novels.

More than 105 years after the supposed beginning of Nofire Hollow, the area was still considered a "country community," a short distance off State Highway 100 and somewhat near Rocky Mountain School in Adair County and Lake Tenkiller in Cherokee County.

Brothers Dennis and Sherman Nofire, natives of Nofire Hollow, said the hollow covered parts of both Adair and Cherokee counties. Dennis, in his late 50s, was a retired canning firm employee living in the Stilwell area. Sherman, in his middle 40s, was a counselor for the Cherokee Nation and lived near Tahlequah.

Meanwhile, Wes Studi, who was in his late 50s, had long been a resident of Santa Fe, New Mexico.

But he was well remembered in his home state.

Once, when in Oklahoma City about four years earlier, he had been honored in the Oklahoma Senate chambers with a citation from then Gov. Frank Keating. The governor declared April 18 as "Wes Studi Day."

And in the hills farther east, many people like brothers Dennis and Sherman continued to be proud of their former neighbor. In Nofire Hollow, no special day was necessary.

Punkin Ridge (circa 1900) – Watermelons, Too

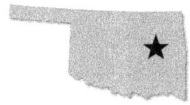

Punkin Ridge is the colloquial name of a pastoral area of blackjack trees, lush pastures and sandy farmland in McIntosh County of eastern Oklahoma. It's believed it was first called Punkin Ridge in 1900 by early settlers to that part of the Creek Nation of Indian Territory.

The name applies to a strip of land bordering Rentiesville in McIntosh County and just south of Oktaha in Muskogee County, and involves the historical areas of part of the old Texas Road, the trail for pioneers heading southwest during the 1800s – which also became a branch of the Shawnee Trail, the first of the long cattle trails out of Texas. The ridge is also the site of the Battle of Honey Springs of Civil War times.

Punkin Ridge is also linked to a few famous names, and is notable among both white and black historians. For years it's been considered a quiet, pastoral place with a pleasant mixture of two cultures.

Also, its name carries a few stories about its origin, all involving one of its traditional crops – although the region in later years became just as well-known for its watermelons.

Punkin Ridge is the home of the late brothers Willard and Benny Combs of rodeo bulldogging fame.

Willard won the world championship in steer wrestling in 1957, and in 2002 was inducted into the National Cowboy & Western Heritage Museum's Rodeo Hall of Fame – but is no more legendary than his onetime bulldogging mare, Baby Doll.

The mare had earned a total of about $400,000 before her sudden death at a Kansas rodeo in 1960. The story of Baby Doll was told in a big spread in *LIFE* magazine.

And tiny Rentiesville, traditionally an all-black community, is the home of historical writer John Hope Franklin; and much later it became the location of the Texas Road Trading Post and Down Home Blues Club, a place nationally known among music lovers of various races.

Roughly 105 years after its surmised beginning, Punkin Ridge was the site of an annual Punkin Ridge Reunion, held in May; a Honey Springs Battlefield Park established by the Oklahoma Historical Society, which also staged re-enactments of the battle every few years; and the Blues Club in Rentiesville.

The park had been established as an educational shrine to the July 17, 1863, battle, during which the Union's 1st Kansas Infantry (Colored) defeated Texas Cavalry soldiers on the Confederate side.

It was the most important Civil War engagement in present-day Oklahoma, partly because it involved Indians on both sides and because it was one of the first battles in that war in which blacks fought as an entire unit.

The Blues Club was operated by 70-year-old D.C. Minner, who had grown up virtually in the same spot. That was where his grandmother, Lura Drennan, once ran the Cozy Corner, a honky-tonk along a dusty road where she sold illegal liquor and homemade "Choc" beer.

Long after he grew up and left for big-city life – in California where he became an accomplished musician – Minner had returned to open his club. He made it into the home of several musical events every year as well as an "Oklahoma Blues Hall of Fame." And it was even uptown enough to have its own Web site.

As to the name "Punkin Ridge," the telling of various stories continued.

One had been repeated by Willard Combs, whose father, Ben, and other relatives came to the area from Missouri. It was the legend of someone finding the shell of a huge pumpkin – with a large sow and her litter of pigs inside.

But Billy Dean Martin, a local rancher in his middle 60s, said the way he heard it, the pumpkin shell housed a few head of cattle.

Dan Lane, another Punkin Ridger in his 60s, said he heard that a pumpkin was discovered in a haystack – "and was so big it took three or four men to put it in a wagon."

Some Oktaha residents suggested the name came from what they saw when they looked southward when the fall foliage was yellow – a ridge the color of a pumpkin.

And other Punkin Ridge memories and stories lived on.

John York, an Oktaha retired teacher in his late 60s, told of a man in Oktaha once known as "Blind Mack" who had said he lost his sight while gambling in the Rentiesville honky-tonk.

York said Mack told it that he was rolling dice, "and he said he was down on his knees, 'and the lights went out!'"

Pumpkins and watermelons had somewhat given way to pastureland along the ridge, but many people still talked about the region's once famous crops.

"It was called Punkin Ridge for as long as I can remember," said James Woods of nearby Checotah, a retired area manager for a national maintenance firm and a native of the area in his middle 70s.

He said that at one time "they had the whole south end of Checotah covered in pumpkins; they were loading them up by the truckloads."

Bob Hill, an Oktaha rancher in his early 80s, said his best memories about Punkin Ridge involved the other product:

"They were always real, real tasty watermelons!"

Roman Nose (circa 1900) – Name with a Face

Roman Nose apparently was the name of a tiny spot of civilization in the early 1900s, and more than three decades later came to designate a popular Oklahoma state park.

According to published reports, Roman Nose was settled as a rural community in Blaine County of Oklahoma Territory in about 1900 (when counties in the territory were designated by names) — and it was the same location of present-day Roman Nose Resort Park.

The park (called Roman Nose State Resort on the official state map), was established in 1936 in Blaine County in the northwestern quarter of Oklahoma.

Its name is from Henry Caruthers Roman Nose, or Wah-Kin-Na, a chief of the Southern Cheyenne Indians who, reportedly from about 1887 to 1917, lived in the canyon that is the site of the present-day park.

And while some historians suggest the name "Roman Nose Canyon" originated earlier – possibly when it was part of the Cheyenne and Arapaho lands of Indian Territory — several sources put the origin of Roman Nose as a place name at around 1900.

Some confusion has also been reported regarding Henry Roman Nose himself, as there is at least one other Roman Nose described in history.

At any rate, it was said Henry Roman Nose expressed his love for his home in the canyon, along with its "spring of everlasting water."

More than 105 years after the apparent beginning of the community of Roman Nose in the present-day Sooner State, Dean Taylor, the Roman Nose park's manager, and others concerned with the park said they found the name fitting and colorful.

M.C. Weber, a 70-year-old retired teacher in Edmond who had authored a book, "Roman Nose, the History of the Park," disagreed with some theories surrounding the name — but called it "very appropriate" as the park's designation.

Leon Hightower, a former longtime manager of the park, agreed the region's place name of Roman Nose probably began about 1900.

Hightower, a retiree in his middle 60s who was living in Weatherford, said a company at Bickford that dealt in gypsum once advertised its "Roman Nose brand" of product.

Bickford reportedly existed about three years after the community of Roman Rose was settled, and only about a mile away. Bickford's post office opened in November 1904, and closed in 1927.

Hightower also said he had always liked the park's name, and so had many of the visitors – for different reasons.

"It drew attention, especially for the horsemen," he said. "They used to say it made them think of 'Roman-nosed horses' – you know, a rounded-face horse."

Texhoma (circa 1901) – A Pair of States

Texhoma, in present-day Texas County of the Oklahoma Panhandle, is believed to have begun as a small settlement in 1901 in what was then Oklahoma Territory. Its post office opened on March 18, 1902.

Texhoma definitely isn't the only place with a name that combines "Texas" and "Oklahoma" (there's also Texola, in Beckham County, which also has been called Texokla and Texoma; and the most popular one of Lake Texoma).

However, Texhoma is considered the only Oklahoma town with that type of name that actually *is* in both the states.

The town is split by the Oklahoma and Texas line, with about two-thirds of the some 1,200 residents on the Oklahoma side.

There are two water towers, two town councils, two mayors, two police departments, two telephone area codes – 580 for Oklahoma and 806 for Texas — and just about two of everything except for the school district and the post office.

And the school district is the only one in Oklahoma divided between two states – where kids start to school in one state and graduate in the other. Grades pre-kindergarten through fourth are in Texas, and grades fifth through 12th are in Oklahoma.

The post office, in Oklahoma, is where all Texhoma residents – on both sides of the state line – come to get their mail.

And the entire downtown area – what there is of it — is in Oklahoma.

It's believed Texhoma began as a very small trade area in the ranch and farm country, on the Oklahoma Territory side, and when it grew it spread over into Texas.

It's also believed the area wasn't without some Oklahoma and Texas rivalry.

According to Ginger Roach, a local historian living over in Texas, Texhoma probably started on the Oklahoma side, "with a little shack that was the post office."

But for a while, she said, "there was quite a bit of competition between the two places."

Around 105 years after Texhoma apparently started, it was still a small town on U.S. 54, with a few businesses and an overall impressive school system on both sides of the border.

Leonard Wright, a longtime resident in his late 50s who was postmaster, said the office, on the Oklahoma side, still served people in both states, and who came and got their mail at their post office boxes.

"The only problem is," he said, "in this new day and age with computers, when not everyone has a ZIP code, sometimes a computer can't find it." He said the ZIP code for Texhoma, Oklahoma, is 73949 – but for people on the Texas side, "they don't have one."

At the Texhoma Auto Supply, Tim Wagner, the 40-year-old manager who was Texhoma's chamber of commerce president, said a question he often hears from travelers is "Where's Lake Texoma?"

He said he and other locals usually have to disappoint the visitors by explaining that it's about 500 miles away.

"Sometimes," he added, "we send 'em out to the sewer pond."

Starvation Creek (circa 1901) – Tough Times?

Starvation Creek, considered a rural community mostly in Beckham County and part of Roger Mills County of western Oklahoma, may have first been called that in the early 1900s, in the region that was then designated as Roger Mills County of Oklahoma Territory.

The name is on a bridge where State Highway 6 crosses the creek between Elk City and Sweetwater.

While residents of the area indicate that it's never been determined how or when Starvation Creek got its name, it has come to be considered a scattered rural community.

One legend has it that a covered wagon of early-day settlers was surrounded by Indians – and during a snowy blizzard in the dead of winter. And the Indians held them at bay for several days "and starved them out."

One report in a newspaper story in 1910 referred to a belief that the creek had some sort of magical or ghostly effect on people who crossed it.

The story had it that "no one ever crossed Starvation Creek without suffering or with the hope of a square meal on the other side."

There are other stories, too – all having to do with hard times in general.

Some 105 years after the area apparently acquired its name, Y.C. Fuchs, a 70-year-old farmer who owned some of the land on both sides of the creek and who lived a few miles west, said the bridge was built in 1948, but the creek had its name long before that.

He said he didn't know how it got its name, but said the stream, which runs into the North Fork of the Red River, crosses a region where "there's not much population."

"If you were a wild animal," he said, "you could easily follow it from the Red River up to the divide north of Grimes and on into the Washita."

Jim Coffey, who lived near the area, said he had heard only vague "stories" about the creek and general region.

"It was before my time," said Coffey, a farmer and rancher and retired educator in his middle 60s. "But I've heard stories about it — stories about a few people that were poor, and got close to starving there."

If things like that happened, it seemed conditions in that area had improved.

Hooker (1902) – Not Really

Hooker, in present-day Texas County of the Oklahoma Panhandle, began as a town in 1902 when that area was Oklahoma Territory. Its post office opened on Oct. 13 of that year.

Hooker is known because of its name and its rather modern-day, somewhat improper connotation – not that town folks have minded all the giggles.

Residents say the town's name, despite some erroneous published reports, was inspired by the reputation of an early-day cattleman, John Threldkeld, who was believed to be the best roper in all of what was then No Man's Land.

It was said that Threldkeld could throw his lasso – and "hook" anything on four legs. He became so famous as "Hooker" Threldkeld that many thought that was his real first name.

Many years later, the word took on another meaning, and outsiders began making jokes – and insiders decided to join in on the fun. It was a great way to promote their community.

"It's a location, not a vocation!" That's been the town slogan, which for a time was on the community's Web site along with the words "The best little town in Oklahoma."

The community advertised and sold T-shirts that said "Hooker Horny Toads" – which for years had been the name of the local American Legion baseball team.

160 / What a Dirty Shame! 101 Unforgettable Place Names of Oklahoma

And there were other T-shirts with such expressions as "Hooker Street Walk"; "Once a Hooker Always a Hooker"; "Not Your Typical Hooker"; "Support Your Local Hookers"; and "All My Friends Are Hookers."

The Hooker joke list went on and on, with cute creations both local and from miles away – and with town promoters probably having more fun than anybody. A special event during its Centennial Celebration was a sharing of "Hooker" stories.

Nearly 105 years after the town's beginning, Hooker, a town of about 1,800 people, continued to promote itself as one of the most joked about places on the national map.

It had drawn national attention, its "vocation" slogan having won a judging of town mottos by Dan Wetzel, sports writer for *Yahoo!*, the Internet directory and communications network.

And "Hooker" was making money.

The "Horny Toad" and other T-shirts had been solicited nationwide, said Claudia Critser, a volunteer with the Hooker Chamber of Commerce. She said people from throughout the nation were buying them, for up to around $15 each, with a passion.

"We send out orders every day or so – we get orders from about everywhere," she said between phone calls. "We have done quite well with our name."

ArVel White, a local civic leader, didn't know exactly when the name of the town began suggesting what it suggests, but recalled the day she heard one of its first snickers.

Several years earlier, while visiting her son on the campus of Oklahoma State University in Stillwater, she was wearing a shirt bearing the words "Hooker School." And she heard the comment of a passing youth: "I didn't know they had schools for that!"

Sheila Blankenship, editor of *The Hooker Advance* newspaper, said that because the jokes from outside were inevitable, "We have to have a sense of humor."

And apparently it was a good thing they did, as even its conventional highway sign caused as many laughs as anything. All it said was "Hooker."

In truth, observers said, Hooker, a decent place with at least eight churches, was one of the most upstanding towns in America. It probably never had a real hooker in its entire history.

Unless, that is, you count Hooker Threldkeld.

Dempsey (1903) – Oklahoma Weather

Dempsey began as a settlement in 1903 in the aforementioned Roger Mills County of Oklahoma Territory, in what would finally become the county by that same name in western Oklahoma. Its post office opened on June 23 of that year.

Dempsey is known for its name, which is possibly linked with famous prizefighter Jack Dempsey; but is particularly remembered because of a storm – one that has been called the classic example of the deadly and uncanny nature of Oklahoma tornadoes.

As to the name, it's been said it came from early-day store owner Web Frankford and wife Hattie, who may have been distant relatives of Jack Dempsey – a possibility, although it would be long before Jack Dempsey was famous in the ring.

The date the local post office was established was one day before Jack Dempsey's birthday of June 24. However, in 1903, Dempsey, who was born in 1895 in Colorado, was only about eight years old, and it was 16 years before he would become world heavyweight boxing champion.

The Dempsey tornado swept through that area the late Wednesday afternoon of May 25, 1955, and was part of a string of twisters that raked sections of Oklahoma, Texas, Kansas and Missouri, killing more than 20 persons in Oklahoma and wrecking some 25 homes in the area.

In the Dempsey area, it dipped down on the Chesney Tidwell farm, instantly killing Chesney and his wife, Bernice, and leaving their 11-year-old son, Wilbert, near death, and with eerie memories that would haunt him forever.

Wilbert was picked up by the giant twister, dropped into a stream, a tributary of West Croton Creek, then swept up into the sky again – and blown over what was left of his family's farm – and finally dropped into a plowed field.

He was found by searchers long after dark, and reported near death, and with most of his body appearing like it had been "sandblasted," then caked with mud.

Five days later when he fully came to in a Sayre hospital, he would remember only confusing bits and pieces of the ordeal.

The first person to arrive at what was left of the Tidwell home after the storm was neighbor Clara Davis. She had driven there as soon as she and her daughter, Linda, had emerged from their dugout. Her husband, Lester, and son, Leon, were away from home when the twister struck.

Many years later Clara would describe the scene at the Tidwell place, where she discovered the bodies of her two longtime friends, "something that I couldn't get out of my mind."

Wilbert Tidwell, after recovering and growing up with relatives, lived in the greater Oklahoma City area and worked for the Federal Aviation Administration.

And because of his experience with the tornado in 1955, he spent many hours as a volunteer tornado spotter.

His memories of the great storm, though vague, could be likened to those of Dorothy in the movie "The Wizard of Oz."

He told of the instant the tornado struck, when "the house just exploded."

"The next thing I knew," he had said, "I was down there in that creek ... sitting down there ... with water all around me."

It was much later when he was told that, during his mumblings before regaining consciousness in the hospital, he described "flying over the barn."

He would often wonder "why was I picked up twice, carried the distance that I was and dropped to the ground twice, and survived to tell about it" – and why his parents were "taken the way they were" and "why was *I* allowed to live?"

Close to 105 years after the beginning of Dempsey, most of what remained of the place was a small community center that had once been the schoolhouse, and a cemetery. The post office had closed in 1913, but it was still on the official state map.

Clara Davis was still among the area residents, and noted they all were proud of the community building, which had been modernized somewhat. And some new words were now on the front of the building, which was built in 1905: "Centennial Dempsey School."

She said area farmers and ranchers were always on the lookout for danger, many times from grassfires and other times violent weather – and she hadn't forgotten the tornado more than 50 years before.

Neither had Wilbert Tidwell, who by now was a man in his early 60s and a resident of Oklahoma City.

Some things had changed for Dempsey people since 1955, but the big storm was often remembered.

America (1903) – More Than a Name

America, once a small but active town in McCurtain County, and in the pine-timbered corner of southeastern Oklahoma, began in 1903 when that region was in the Choctaw Nation of Indian Territory. Its post office opened on July 24 of that year.

Historical records say it was named for Americus Stewart, wife of pioneer resident Tom Stewart – who himself was the namesake of the nearby town of Tom, which began several years later than America.

However, the community of America is remembered not only because of its name but, fittingly, its patriotic spirit – as well as its ironic ending.

It's been said that the local patriotism actually brought about the town's demise, which happened during World War II.

The late Bob Green, considered an authority on the area, had insisted the town of America died solely because of the war.

"You had the war come on, and the younger people left, and them that didn't go to war went to defense plants," he said, explaining that he was among those who did the latter.

"At that time everybody was needed," was the way he put it. "Support the country – that's what people were thinking of."

Green said when the war ended, he was one of the few who returned to America, and the place soon dwindled away.

More than a century after the beginning of the town of America, virtually no sign of it was visible, and some residents of that area didn't seem to know such a place had ever existed. Its post office had closed in 1944.

One who did remember America, however, was Willie Mae Clowers, a native of the area who lived at nearby Tom. She recalled the final days of the town of America – as well as when she lost a husband in the war.

"Seemed like it just went out overnight," she said about the community of America. It was also about that time that her Army soldier husband, George Leon Baker, was killed in action.

Clowers, who later remarried, also had memories of her childhood in America, concerning both its remote location and its name.

She recalled that, as young Willie Mae Fairless, she and other youngsters used to visit a brush arbor deeper in the woods, where her cousin was once bitten by a venomous snake – and recovered, but only after "she swole up like a balloon. If you'd stuck a pin in her, she'd a busted."

And Willie Mae said when she attended school in Idabel, some 15 miles away, a teacher refused to believe her when she reported her birthplace as "America, Oklahoma."

Bugtussle (1903) – 'Little Giant'

Bugtussle began as the name of a rural school built of logs in 1903 in the Choctaw Nation of Indian Territory, the area that would become part of Pittsburg County of southeastern Oklahoma.

The name, partly because of its funny sound, is considered one of the most memorable in the state.

However, for many residents it's unforgettable because it immediately brings to mind the name of the late Carl Albert, the native of Bugtussle who became speaker of the U.S. House and finally known throughout the state as "the Little Giant from Little Dixie."

Albert, remembered for going from a humble rural beginning to reaching the highest government post of any Oklahoman, died in 2000 at age 91.

It's believed that Bugtussle, which for years was a two-room school on a wooded hilltop and was also known as Flowery Mound, acquired its original name of Bugtussle from one of the builders of the first school building, which was made of logs.

It was once told by W.K. "Bill" Anderson, the county superintendent of schools – who also went to Bugtussle School — that Ran Woods, who helped build the small schoolhouse, "complained all the time about how hard it was to keep the bugs down," and "it was his idea to call it 'Bugtussle.'"

Close to 105 years after Bugtussle was named, it was a community of a few hundred people – and considered a quiet place to live that retained its historical attraction.

Visitors occasionally came, apparently to see what Bugtussle looked like, according to Denise Brannon. She and her husband, Gaylon, a college teacher in his late 40s, had lived there for some 25 years.

As for the famous old schoolhouse, she said, "the old building is still there."

And to many Oklahomans, the small structure was the supreme symbol of the man called "the Little Giant."

Okesa (circa 1905) – Unforgettable Elmer

Okesa may have begun in 1905 as a settlement along Sand Creek in the Osage Nation of Oklahoma Territory, its post office opening on Jan. 17, 1906. It would soon become part of Osage County of northeastern Oklahoma, the state's largest county as well as a region often referred to as "the Osage."

Okesa is an Osage word meaning "halfway," and it was so named because of its being halfway between Pawhuska and the boundary of the Cherokee Nation.

However, it also was the site of several train robberies of yesteryear, and is probably best known as the place where train robber Elmer McCurdy began the long and most unusual saga that made him world famous — posthumously speaking.

It was near Okesa where on a rainy night in early October of 1911, McCurdy, about 32, and a few cohorts – their horses tied nearby and with pistols blazing – held up a train on the MK&T (Katy) Railroad. They had hopped on the train when it ran slowly through a "cut" to pull the holdup, about 1 a.m., Oct. 4.

A few days after the luckless robbery — it netted the bandits about $45 and some whiskey — McCurdy was cornered where he was holed up in a barn near Pawhuska and shot and killed by an Osage County posse on Oct. 7, 1911, a Saturday.

At that time McCurdy's mummified body began undergoing a series of nearly incredible circumstances before it was discovered some 65 years later being used as a side-show dummy in California.

It was then brought back to Oklahoma – along considerable publicity — and buried in the Boot Hill section of the Summit View Cemetery in Guthrie.

Then, some 26 years later, the bizarre story of Elmer was given more fanfare when it was featured on national television. Much of it was re-enacted and dramatized for a program on Point TV.

McCurdy's body had first been embalmed with arsenic at a Pawhuska funeral home, and reportedly was taken by someone claiming to be a relative. It apparently didn't resemble a human corpse, and wound up being displayed at various side shows for many years and finally, after being covered with fluorescent paint, became a prop on the TV series, "Six-Million-Dollar Man."

It was finally discovered, as the body of a real person, in a Long Beach, California, carnival fun house in December 1976.

Ralph McCalmont, then a Guthrie civic leader, and Fred Olds, an artist and onetime director of the Oklahoma Territorial Museum in Guthrie, went to Los Angeles to arrange for the return of McCurdy's body.

Dr. Clyde Snow, noted forensic anthropologist of Norman, also went to California to assist in identifying the body.

McCurdy, a native of Maine who had come west in about 1900, had never become more than a small-time criminal.

However, McCalmont, who later became director of the state's Tourism and Recreation Department, said that while McCurdy was a failure as a bandit, "it's his afterlife that made him so darn important."

And Snow said McCurdy "in his first life was a total loser, but in his second life he was a smashing success" – even though he didn't have the best name to become a famous outlaw.

Snow said that if the bandit had ever stomped up to a teller's window, with pistols drawn, and said "'I'm Elmer McCurdy!' – they'd laugh him out of the bank."

More than 100 years after Okesa's beginning, the community was comprised of one or two businesses or public buildings, and some scattered homes. The post office had closed in 1940, but the place remained on the state map.

Frances Gardner, a longtime area resident who said she lived "on top of the hill over Okesa," said the place was "very small – there's a bar and the fire department, and that's about it."

She said she was aware of the area's history of train robberies, apparently including holdups that occurred there even later than the one involving Elmer McCurdy. "I think it's noted for having the last one. It was notorious."

"There's a lot of history here," she added. "I've always said someone ought to write a book about Okesa."

Vamoosa (1906) – 'That Name Will Do!'

Vamoosa, in the southern part of present-day Seminole County of Oklahoma, began in 1906 in what was then the Seminole Nation of Indian Territory. Its post office was established on May 19 of that year.

While not all historians agree on how the community started, it's generally believed its name comes from the English word derived from the early American mispronunciation of the Spanish term *vámonos,* meaning "let's go."

About a century after Vamoosa began, the community mainly consisted of a well-kept cemetery along State Highway 99, with a monument at the gate paying honors to pioneer resident and landowner John P. Vance; two churches – the Vamoosa Baptist and the Grace Community, the latter adjoining the vacated old brick school building — and a few scattered homes east of the highway.

The local post office had closed in 1918.

As to "Vamoosa," Kevin Duck, a resident in his middle 30s who was pastor of the Baptist house of worship, repeated the legend – that the name resulted from a remark during a long, tiring formal get-to-

gether of settlers inside what was probably the first building there.

Arthur Kennedy of nearby Konawa, a retired history teacher in his middle 80s, said Vamoosa wasn't settled by any particular person and never became much of a place — "but at one time it had a large school, and it was known for its basketball."

However, he said he had never heard the story that Kevin Duck told about the community's name:

"The way I heard it," the minister said, "they were having a meeting, and couldn't decide what to name it (the new settlement). And finally, someone said 'Well, let's vamoose out of here!'"

The name obviously stuck — and was still remembered for at least 100 years after those people vamoosed and went home.

Saint Louis (circa 1906) – Joking Around

Saint Louis, a tiny town in present-day Pottawatomie County of Oklahoma, probably acquired its name in 1906 when it was part of the county of Pottawatomie, Oklahoma Territory.

That's according to what many observers consider the most likely origin of "Saint Louis" – despite the fact its post office didn't open under that name until March 22, 1928, and even if part of its name is spelled "St." on road signs and on the official state map.

While there's another – and more romantic – legend behind the name, the more popular story is that it came from a witty remark by a local rural schoolteacher, comparing the quiet little place to the large city in Missouri.

It's said that the teacher, Sam Johnson, was either walking or riding a horse toward the tiny settlement, then called Simpsonville, when someone asked him where he was heading.

He smiled, the story goes, and answered "Oh, I'm just going into St. Louis."

The name caught on, and finally became official, but with the first part spelled out.

About 100 years after Saint Louis apparently got its name, the community, which once had been an active trade center in an area of farming and oilfield activity, had dwindled to a small place with the hint of a business district. A few new public structures gave it a mixture of the modern and the ramshackle.

And it seemed most of the local people – including postmaster Lonnie Courtney and Mayor Sue Goodnight - agreed the town's name was from the schoolteacher's lighthearted remark.

So did Mildred Dennis, a resident of Perry, Ohio, who as young Mildred Murphy lived in the Saint Louis area during the 1930s and 40s.

She wrote a book about her former home called "It's Gonna Be OK – A Lease Child's Legacy."

Mildred did cite the other legend: That once some Texas cowboys who were driving a herd to Missouri, being lost after a heavy rainstorm, approached the little settlement of Simpsonville, and one of them said, "Well, I guess we finally got to St. Louis."

But she said the most accepted theory involved the remark by the rural teacher, when "he was just joking around."

Meanwhile, along with the standard road signs – and apparently in the true tradition of a town with a sense of humor about names — was a billboard-type greeting at the edge of town. It described Saint Louis as the home of "179 Friendly People," but also of one "pyromaniac" and a "busybody."

And Mayor Goodnight, who acknowledged she had authored the funny phrase, explained that "pyromaniac" applied to a real person – "a man who used to burn trash."

The other term, she said, referred to "just about everybody here – you know, we're a small town."

Wild Horse Mountain (circa 1906) – Barbecue Country

Wild Horse Mountain may have been named shortly before 1907 in what was then the southern part of the Cherokee Nation of Indian Territory. It became a landmark in what eventually was Sequoyah County of eastern Oklahoma – and where the term is probably best known because of barbecue.

According to the legend, possibly just before statehood, a young Indian man – either Cherokee or possibly Choctaw from the nation to the south – was chasing a fast horse that had gotten loose in the rugged, hilly region, until he finally captured it in a very unconventional manner.

However, the name is probably best known because of an eating establishment at the foot of the timbered rise – the Wild Horse Mountain Bar-B-Que, for many years an informal, open-air place operated by Hubert and Betty Holman.

A century after the legend of the spirited horse is believed to have begun, Wild Horse Mountain Bar-Be-Que, south of Sallisaw along U.S. Highway 59, was still operating after some 40 years — though slightly modernized from its original picnic table and alfresco setting. It was managed by brothers Bill and Dale Holman and their sister, Cathy Fine.

Bill Holman knew the wild horse legend well:

"The way I heard it, there was an Indian boy trying to chase down a wild horse for somebody, and he finally shot it with a rifle, and it grazed its spinal cord – he was a good shot. It didn't hurt the horse, and he caught 'im."

"I've heard that story from the old-timers over and over," said Bill, a man in his late 40s.

And he figured he'd keep telling it, over and over.

Moonshine Road (circa 1907) – Spirited Memories

Moonshine Road, in the wooded hills of eastern Oklahoma, is a drive that links State Highway 82 near the rural community of Box and U.S. Highway 64 near Gore in Sequoyah County.

Besides being known for its colorful name, it's significant because it leads to the religious ceremonial grounds of the Redbird Smith Nighthawk Keetoowah Society – a sacred shrine to the Cherokee Nation.

As to Moonshine Road itself, it's believed the 10-mile stretch acquired its name shortly after statehood in 1907, when Oklahoma gained the reputation of becoming the first state to enter the nation dry – resulting in a bustling business in bootlegged booze.

Both Indian Territory, where liquor was already illegal, and Oklahoma Territory, where the saloon business was wide open, had both become officially dry by an election two months before the two territories became a state.

After prohibition went into effect on statehood day of Nov. 16, 1907, according to a story in *The Sunday Oklahoman*, ". bootleggers did not operate as flamboyantly as gangsters in Chicago and other big cities, but it was general knowledge that a lot of grain in Oklahoma was not used to make flour or corn meal, nor was it fed to livestock."

And the then-unpaved road was a major route for traffickers of illegal liquor – plus it cut right through the whiskey peddlers' home country.

It's been said that Moonshine Road was the heart of both a place and time that gave birth to the expression, "So many people were selling whiskey they had to put up signs to keep from selling it to each other."

Nearly 100 years after Oklahoma's statehood and prohibition, Moonshine Road was still designated at one end, although the sign at the road's junction of highway 64 was gone – apparently the work of souvenir hunters.

Meanwhile, tales of Moonshine Road and area lived on.

Dennis Jackson, a rural Gore resident, said his grandfather, Sampson Still, a Cherokee, lost his life to liquor-related violence.

Jackson, a retired oil company technician in his late 60s, said Still, who carried a pistol, liked people to drink with him when he was drinking – "and if someone wouldn't drink with him, he'd get mad and pull out the ol' hog leg."

Dennis said that apparently happened and caused a ruckus one day many years ago in downtown Gore, and his grandfather was then chased into a nearby cornfield by a posse – of either lawmen or vigilantes – and shot and killed.

But to E.L. Poteete of Webbers Falls, a retired merchant also in his late 60s, the famous old road had fonder connotations.

He said his late wife, Erma Renfro Poteete, grew up along Moonshine Road, where her parents ranched between there and the nearby Illinois River. And he often recalled when he was "a frequent visitor into that area to call on my wife to be."

However, Poteete said he also knew many people in that region who used to produce the moonshine — but he didn't name them, since "some of 'em are still livin', and lots of 'em, their grandchildren still live around here."

But regardless of what outsiders might think, according to Gene Risley, a longtime resident of rural Gore, at one time people near Moonshine Road practically considered that activity a part of farming.

"They was all moonshiners back in there. They made whiskey and had cattle and hogs – that was their livin'," said Risley, a rancher and retired construction worker in his late 70s.

"When they wasn't in the field," he said, "they was makin' liquor."

Medicine Spring (circa 1909) – Gilbert's 'Hidalgo'

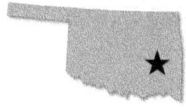

Medicine Spring, which became a recognized area in the timbered hills of Pushmataha County of southeastern Oklahoma, is believed to have been named a few years after statehood when someone carried a crippled man to the spring, which was said to be healthful.

According to the legend, the man, whose name may have been Daniels – since at first the place was called Daniels' Spring – was revitalized by the water, so built a log house and stayed.

Soon, others came for the reported therapeutic benefits of the water, and by the early 1930s, when it was known as Medicine Spring, it was a health resort with a large hotel and a rock enclosure where the spring spilled into a concrete basin.

The health resort gradually dwindled away, and for several years the remote region was the inspiration for stories of hidden treasure, and became better known as Medicine Spring Ranch.

The ranch was operated by Gilbert Jones, a seasoned cowboy who for some 30 years lived in a house virtually without electricity or other modern conveniences and raised horses, including many that freely roamed the pine-covered hills. He also served as chairman of a group he called the Southwest Spanish Mustang Association.

More than 95 years after the reported beginning of Medicine Spring, the area, a few miles east of Finley, was the site of some logging operations and occasional church revival meetings.

It also was the headquarters for organized horseback rides and competitions a few times every year – as a tribute to Gilbert Jones, who at age 94 had died about five years earlier.

And Jones was remembered throughout much of the country where horses are popular, and the kind of horses that he fancied were remembered as well.

Many people near Medicine Spring especially were quick to mention that Gilbert Jones was listed on the screen at the end of the movie "Hidalgo," and credited as having one of the last herds of mustangs in the nation.

Loretta Tabor, the Finley postmaster, said the many local horsemen and the movie people had been there a few years earlier during part of the filming.

But movies or not, she said Jones was well remembered throughout much of southeastern Oklahoma:

"I guess everybody around, knew Gilbert."

Strong City (circa 1911) – Firewater Express

Strong City apparently was settled sometime in 1911 along a bend of the Washita River in Roger Mills County of western Oklahoma. Its post office opened on Sept. 26 of 1912.

While its name, from railroad developer Clinton Strong, is considered noteworthy, the town is better remembered as the site of one of the most ambitious bootlegging schemes in history – and especially because of the plan's grand fiasco.

During the 1920s, four local men – barber Hoyt Little and businessmen O.T. "Pete" Girdner, H.T. Banner and Francis Walker – reportedly arranged to have some 200 gallons of alcohol, packed inside about 34,000 pounds of iced-down cabbage, smuggled in by rail from Mexico.

But a federal man somehow got wind of it, and stationed himself incognito in Strong City to wait on the train.

But the four conspirators somehow got wind of the federal man, so after the train arrived wouldn't go near the boxcar, which had been placed to a side track.

After a few days of the standoff, the federal man and local lawmen, armed with axes, opened the boxcar and chopped through the smelly cabbage to the containers of liquid – most of which spilled into the streets.

And as men and boys began dipping up the spirits from puddles here and there, someone struck and dropped a match. In seconds, the depot was on fire.

It was Saturday, Jan. 26, 1929, and would be talked about for years as the day Strong City was filled with smoke, shouts of alarm, laugher and overall pandemonium.

Several months later, the four local suspects were indicted by a federal grand jury in Brownsville, Texas, and tried for smuggling, but acquitted.

And although no money was made on the deal, the imported booze didn't go to waste.

Years later, Earl Archer, a retired Strong City railroad worker who had witnessed the whole affair, said authorities barely saved enough of the alcohol for evidence.

He said they tried to save a five-gallon can and a fruit jar of it – "and someone stole the five-gallon can."

Nearly 95 years after Strong City began, its post office had long been closed, and the town consisted of little more than a community building, a few homes and its large but rusty water tower.

At nearby Cheyenne, Shirley Whitson, daughter of the late Earl Archer, said she seldom heard remarks anymore about the big 1929 event witnessed by her father – but when she did, she enjoyed discussing it.

"It's a very interesting story," she said.

Ragtown (1913) – Tents, Shacks and Peddlers

Ragtown was a town in Carter County of southern Oklahoma that looked like it had gone up overnight – which it had.

It was a shabby bunch of shacks and tents where oil-field workers could eat, sleep and spend all their money on wide-open fun.

While all that may be an exaggeration – though some historians say it isn't – it's one description of the place that has been called a model of the state's petroleum industry.

Ragtown began in 1913 following a major oil well discovery, and was the forerunner of Wirt, named for oilman Wirt Franklin. Wirt's post office opened on Dec. 12, 1914, and that town would eventually become part of Healdton.

Ragtown, besides being associated with the Healdton-Hewitt Oil Field, was called a center for "whiskey and wild women" and a lawless, dangerous place.

It's believed it was so named because of its many tents at one time — but another story is about traveling salesmen.

Marilyn Smith Curtis, a resident of Duncan who was familiar with the Ragtown area, once told of reports of "peddlers, who had strips of cloth for sale – and they were called 'rag men.'"

Nearly 95 years after Ragtown began, its only reminders were a few old structures at the west edge of Healdton. The Wirt post office had long been closed.

Kenneth Eck, a local resident who wrote a regular column called "Oil Patch Mania" for the *Healdton Herald*, said the old community's many tents had something to do with several fires over the years.

"Those old shacks, you know, were just thrown together," said Eck, a retired pharmacist in his late 80s. And when they burned, and until more building was done, he said, "people would put up more tents."

Titanic (circa 1915) – Unsinkable?

Titanic is a tiny community in Adair County of eastern Oklahoma that for many years has kept its identity – though barely.

It apparently began sometime in 1915 as a store amid a small settlement. Its post office opened on Jan. 3 of 1916.

It's believed the store was operated by Bart Dick, who also was the first postmaster. Others who ran the business over the years included I.Z. Coleman and Kay Stewart.

The name Titanic apparently came from local conversations about the sinking of the ocean liner Titanic about three years before – on April 15, 1912.

Many years after the community was officially gone, Lillian Stewart, Kay Stewart's wife, had said the tragic event at sea was still on the minds of many at that time — "everybody was talking about that ship sinking."

More than 90 years after the apparent beginning of Titanic, the place, about 12 miles northwest of Stilwell, was still considered a rural community, but was little more than the vacated store building, a church and a cemetery. Its post office had closed in 1927.

Still living there was Pat Woodward and her husband, Clarence. Pat, granddaughter of the late Stewarts, said she had been told the name of the place specifically resulted from comments about the Titanic by one of the store's first customers.

"A man came in, and he was so concerned with that, and just kept talking about it," she said, "so it was named because of this one person."

Sharon Treib, a resident of the nearby Spade Mountain area, as well as a staff member of the Adair County Historical Society in Stilwell, said the name Titanic had virtually become forgotten – but not quite.

It was the name of a business – Titanic Upholstery – a short distance from the rural community on State Highway 51.

Florene Gass, the owner, said she chose that name when she launched her enterprise some 20 years before, after others cast doubt on its success.

She said she told them "Well, I'm gonna name it Titanic, and when it goes under I'll just say 'the Titanic sunk again.'"

But so far, she said, it was still afloat.

Salt Springs (1920) – Racing for Dollars

Salt Springs began as a bustling little trade center in the middle of the Selman Ranch in Harper County of western Oklahoma, and didn't last long – but left a colorful past.

It's remembered because of its name – for a nearby spring of undrinkable water – but more so for being called the only town in the state where a horse race and bank robbery overlapped. It would become one of the most laughed about incidents in history.

Salt Springs, with little more than a railroad stop, cattle-loading chute, bank, grain elevator and store, officially began as a post office on June 3, 1920.

Its big day came nearly a year later – reportedly on March 30, 1921, a Tuesday – when a horse race was scheduled as part of a celebration.

Just as the some 80 nervous horses and riders were lined up and waiting, the gunshot they heard wasn't the starting signal – a holdup was taking place!

Local banker A.C. Clothier, bloodied up from a blow to the head and calling for help, came rattling and bumping toward the waiting horse racers in his Model T Ford automobile.

And the bandits, apparently a gang of them — also on horseback – were flying out of town in swirls of dust.

One of the local horsemen yelled "Look, there they go yonder!"

Another hollered "Let's get 'em!"

And the race, you might say, was on.

Amid both screams of alarm and cheers from the crowd, the local good guys were off. They bunched their horses up and thundered over the narrow wooden bridge that crossed Buffalo Creek – then, in a blur of speed, were gone over a rise of sagebrush and sand plums, after the desperadoes.

But the robbers had the loot in a sack, which came open during their flight. And the money was recovered by the unusual posse who, one by one, reined up and dismounted to pick up the scattered bills and change.

The bandits, with empty sack, escaped.

But the culprits — Joseph Heirholzer, Bennett Highfill, Thomas Dickson and Charles Brankel – were soon nabbed by lawmen and convicted in district court at Buffalo and sent to jail for 10 years.

The whole incident later was described by Bob Selman, who at eight years old, with his horse, Max, had been the youngest of the racers.

It turned out that the stolen money – said to total $258.25 – had been recovered and turned in by the local brave and honest heroes.

Well, almost.

Selman said that after it was counted, what he and the others had gathered on the prairie didn't quite tally up:

"We got all the money back but six cents."

More than 85 years after Salt Springs began, it was long gone. Its post office had closed in 1928. About all that was left at the site, east of Buffalo and south of the Cimarron River, were a few foundations and pieces of corrals and rotted railroad ties.

Sue Selman of Woodward, daughter of the late Bob Selman and owner of the ranch, called the spot "one of my favorite places to go." She also was among the authors of a book, "Buffalo Creek Chronicles."

However, she said, "it's hard to imagine anyone ever living out there." And she found it hard to believe anyone ever had:

"The water was pure salt."

Babbs Switch (circa 1920) – A Christmas Tragedy

Babbs Switch is believed to have begun in about 1920 as a store and service station operated by Matt Braun along an unpaved highway six miles south of Hobart in Kiowa County of southwestern Oklahoma.

While the origin of "Babbs Switch" isn't clear, it's speculated that the name comes from an early settler named Babcock and a signal and stop on the Frisco Railroad.

The tiny community would later include a grain elevator, a rodeo ground and a small schoolhouse.

It was the schoolhouse that, on Christmas Eve of 1924, became the site of one of the most heartbreaking disasters in the history of the nation.

The tiny frame building was packed. It was the beginning of the community's big Christmas tree program. Gifts and sacks of apples, oranges, nuts and candy were under the large cedar tree that had been cut and brought in and made a thing of beauty, adorned with burning candles.

At the height of the program, Santa Claus, played by 17-year-old Dow Bolding, accidentally bumped one of the branches of the tree. A candle fell.

It would later be described as an explosion of fire, and a scene of scrambling panic and screams of indescribable pain as an estimated 150 people stampeded against the door, which was virtually impossible to pull open against the frenzied jam of humanity.

While some managed to get out, many remained trapped inside the inferno of agony.

Among the first to burn to death was the young Dow Bolding. His was one of 36 lives claimed by the fire.

Many of the bodies were impossible to identify.

Others who somehow escaped the building were horribly scared, their lives never to be the same, both physically and mentally.

Twenty of the victims were buried in a mass grave in the Hobart Cemetery.

Eighty-five years later, one of the few living survivors of the fire was Lillie Braun, a resident of Hobart in her late 80s.

She could describe only "flashes" of memory of the night when, as Lillie Biggers, only a few years old, "I crawled out from under a desk and I went behind Momma . . . and I drug my doll out."

She also recalled hearing "the screaming above me."

Her mother, Margaret Biggers, also survived the fire, but was seriously injured.

Her two older brothers, Walter and William Biggers, died in the fire.

Joe Hebensperger, 96, also of Hobart, who was 11 at the time, had fled the building at the start of the fire, and over the years had told relatives "how the fire spread so terribly fast," according to his son, Jim Hebensperger.

Lillie Braun said she has never had bad dreams about the fire.

"I don't know if I blocked it out of my head or what," she said, but added: "Every time I see fire, I remember it. I'm scare to death of fires"

The Babbs Switch School, possibly a year or two before the fire. Photo courtesy, The Oklahoman.

Because the school had only one main door, which opened only to the inside, the incident led to new state regulations aimed at making public buildings safer, with guidelines saying all doors should open to the outside.

But that didn't erase some sad memories of the Christmas Eve fire in a country schoolhouse.

Some 89 years after Babbs Switch began, on the site of the one-time community was a monument telling of the 1924 schoolhouse fire and a picnic table along U.S. Highway 183.

The site was also on the official state map as Babbs.

Bill Williams of Hobart, president of the Kiowa County Historical Society, said local people and visitors alike continued to talk about the Babbs Switch fire.

"It was a terrible, terrible thing," he said — "one of the most terrible tragedies that ever happened in Oklahoma."

Pie Flat (circa 1920) – Sweet Things

Pie Flat, a quiet spec of civilization a little south of the Canadian River in Roger Mills County of western Oklahoma, may have started from the talk of bashful country boys.

Apparently the community, of a few homes scattered around and a tiny, well-kept cemetery, started as a settlement with a one-room school. It's been estimated the place had been established as Pie Flat by around 1920.

More than 85 years after the estimated beginning of Pie Flat, the place, situated north of Roll, appeared like time had done little to change it, except that the school had long been gone.

Wayne Barber, a local rancher, said the community's name possibly was the result of typical rural courtship.

Barber, an area native in his early 70s, said he had been told some young men from a few miles away once had the custom of often visiting a certain family.

"They used to ride their horses over here," he said. "And they would say it was because the mother of the family 'made real good pies.'"

However, he said, "some people thought the boys liked to see the girls, and that 'pies' was a good excuse."

Wizzbang (1921) – Boomtown

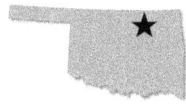

Wizzbang was the local name for a town that sprang up in Osage County in northeastern of Oklahoma during one of the state's large oil-producing eras of the 1920s. Its official name was Denoya, and its post office opened on Dec. 31, 1921.

While there are multiple stories – some of them quite earthy — about why it was called Wizzbang, a popular belief is that it was named for *Captain Billy's Whiz Bang,* a humor magazine especially popular in the 1920s.

Wizzbang (also sometimes spelled Whizbang) apparently came about with the opening of the Burbank Oil Field, and is remembered not only for its unique and humorous name, but its reputation as one of the wildest Oklahoma boomtowns.

Like Ragtown, for a time Wizzbang was a settlement of numerous tents and hastily built frame houses, along with countless illegal liquor houses and brothels. Reports of killings and robberies in the street and various other acts of orneriness were many.

Wizzbang was remembered long after its heyday by Blue Starr, a farmer and stockman who lived in another part of the county.

He once said that as a boy he had to run errands on horseback, "and a man used to tell me: 'When you get to Wizzbang, gallop that horse!'" Starr said the man "was afraid I'd get caught in the crossfire of a shootin' match."

Some historians even say Clark Gable, who years later would become a top Hollywood actor, may have visited Wizzbang with his father. Gable, a native of Ohio, worked with his father, Will, in the Osage County oil fields during the early '20s.

Oddly, after Gable became a star of the silver screen, among his many roles was in a movie about the oil fields, called "Boom Town."

Some 85 years after the beginning of Wizzbang, except for the soft thumping of a pump jack, there was virtually no sign of the onetime wild town. The Denoya post office had closed in 1942.

Marlene Fields, editor of *The Review* newspaper at nearby Shidler, said there were "a few houses out there, and that's about all."

"I couldn't even find the old jail," she said, referring to the remnants of a stone building considered symbolic of old rowdy Wizzbang. "They say it's there somewhere, but I never could find it."

Tater Hill (circa 1924) – Dizzy Dean

Tater Hill is called that because of one of the many stories about Dizzy Dean:

When he was a youngster living near Spaulding, in Hughes County of eastern Oklahoma, there was one particular hill near his family's house where he liked to exercise his throwing arm. He would throw a potato over the hill and run around the other side and catch it.

Like many tales by, and about, the late Dizzy Dean, the onetime famous baseball pitcher turned sports announcer, that anecdote isn't taken seriously. Nevertheless, Tater Hill became the local name of the rural area where Dean lived as a boy.

Dean, whose real name may have been Jay Hanna Dean or Jerome Herman Dean, was born in Arkansas, in about 1910, but his home at one time was near Spaulding. His father, Monroe Dean, was a sharecropper.

According to Johnny Mayfield, a Spaulding merchant and former mayor who started an annual Dizzy Dean Day in the early 1990s, it was believed Dean went to high school there in the mid-1920s – "and someone said the only time he came to school was when they had a baseball game."

Dean became a professional baseball pitcher and won 30 games when he pitched the St. Louis Cardinals to a World Series title in 1934. He won a place in baseball's Hall of Fame in 1953.

Following an injury, Dean, who at some point picked up the "Dizzy" nickname, became a baseball radio and television commentator with a style so easy-going and unsophisticated it was plumb unique.

It was said Dizzy drew complaints to the Federal Communications Commission with some of his improper English – like saying a player "slud into third" or another "threwed" the ball. He also would say a good batter could be "mighty hitterish."

When broadcasting football, he called officials "those guys wearin' striped pajamas."

Dean reportedly told it that he only finished the second grade, and that "I didn't do so good in the first grade, either."

It's said he once responded to criticism for his use of "ain't" by saying "A lot of folks that ain't sayin' 'ain't' ain't eatin.'"

And Spaulding area residents came to consider Dean a favorite son, and were proud that he remembered his former home in Oklahoma.

They were especially jubilant when Dean, while announcing a game on radio or TV, would mention something about "Tater Hill."

More than 80 years after Tater Hill apparently got its name, the area where Dean and his family once lived remained wooded and quiet.

However, Spaulding's 13th annual Dizzy Dean Day, usually held sometime in October, was being planned with gusto, said Johnny Mayfield, who by this time was a local merchant in his late 40s.

And the name Tater Hill had become a big part of the yearly celebration.

Just outside Mayfield's business, the Spaulding Feed & Supply, was a collection of Dizzy Dean memorabilia under the sign "Tater Hill."

Also, Mayfield said the community was proud of its own baseball team – and especially its name: "the Tater Hillbillies."

Dirty Shame (circa 1925) – A Lovely Landmark

Dirty Shame, at a southwestern Oklahoma crossroads amid wheat fields and mesquite pastures and within sight of the Wichita Mountains, apparently began in 1925 as a gasoline station and store a few years after first being known as Carter's Station.

It would eventually become a vacated store building six miles south of Carnegie in Caddo County, at the corner of State Highway 58 and a county road.

As to how the place got its name, it's doubtful any two people will agree. But the consensus is that an unabashed observation was once

Dirty Shame, when it operated as a business, circa 1982.

made about something – or somebody – to the effect of "ain't that a dirty shame!"

One story, told several years back by area farmer Norris Scrudder, is that a female employee at the station – who was rather short – once needed to get some water for an overheated car radiator, and tried to dip a bucket into a 55-gallon water barrel. But she fell over into it, headfirst.

And, Scrudder said, while the woman "was there with her legs sticking out, kickin', the ol' boy that ran the place, who was about half lit all the time, just laughed and said 'Ain't that a dirty shame!'"

Another account, by David Whisenhunt, a former manager of the station, has it that an outspoken woman who once ran the place got her dander up when a passing truck caused a rock to thud on the store's tin roof — but she blamed it on a passing pedestrian.

"She ran out and cussed the ol' boy out," Whisenhunt said. He added that spectators who were standing around commented how wrong of her it was, "cussin' that poor man" – and how, of course, it was a dirty shame.

Other stories ranged from ones linked with rivalry between the station and an earlier business across the road; to some youngsters who had the measles; and to a residence virtually hidden by a pile of junk.

Some 80 years after it apparently was named, area residents said the place still had an identity – with even some mail being sent to "Dirty Shame, OK."

And as to the stories about the name, according to Darrell Schmidt, a farmer in his early 60s who owned the old Dirty Shame store building, "there's a lot of 'em – it's just about whatever you want to make up."

He and his wife, Phyllis, had also operated the store in the early 1990s, and later considered tearing the building down – until, Phyllis said, "we had an uprising!" Area residents didn't want to see it go.

"People still talk about it all the time," she said. "When giving directions, they'll say things like 'six miles to Dirty Shame.' Everybody in Caddo County and many from Kiowa County know where Dirty Shame is."

She said she once had a Web site that she called "Dirty Shame Lady," plus had ball caps with the name on them — "and people from Germany and everywhere else would call and want my ball caps."

Eugene Zimmerman, an area resident in his late 70s, said he had one of the caps, too, and once took it on a trip to California.

"I wore it on the airplane," he said, "and people kept lookin' at it and wanted to know where was Dirty Shame at."

The name has also been popular with a group of Comanche Indians living in the vicinity, who once named their dancing group — who used rattling gourds along with feather fans, sashes and the like — the "Dirty Shame Gourd Club."

While the club included other members representing tribes such as the Kiowas and Apaches and from other communities, originators of the group considered the name good medicine.

Also, as Herbie Pewo, one of the group's dancers in his late 20s, once said, "It's just the name of our community."

Ron Thompson, a man in his early 50s who was living in the former store building and caring for it, said it remained a popular spot for farmers to gather and visit, and that other people "stop by and take pictures every so often."

He said the old "Dirty Shame" name on the building had faded, so he decided to repaint it.

He figured it'd be a shame not to.

Ticky Ridge (circa 1925) – Itchy Subjects

Ticky Ridge is the local name for a rural area in Adair County of eastern Oklahoma that probably acquired its odious nickname in 1925.

Ticky Ridge lies roughly between Westville and Christie and past Peacheater Creek toward the Chance community.

It's believed Ticky Ridge was first called that in the middle 1920s, apparently during a time when the tiny bloodsucking insects were especially bad.

And while modern agriculture has done much to control all insects in recent years, and that area, along with the entire state, has changed, the name Ticky Ridge apparently has long been embedded in local memories.

Several years ago a local dairy farmer and feed dealer, Sam Langley, recalled a time when his parents talked about "shingle ticks."

"The ticks would be on top of one another on a cow or horse," he said, "and you had to rake 'em off with a currycomb, and then pour kerosene on 'em."

More than 80 years after Ticky Ridge apparently was first called that, much of the area had a pleasant look of pastures cleared of brush and neat farm homes, and the name Ticky Ridge wasn't mentioned much anymore.

But it wasn't forgotten.

Sam Langley, who by this time was in his early 70s and was a general farmer and feed dealer, said the place had been called several things in recent years.

"That name kinda went out several years ago," he said of Ticky Ridge, explaining that people called it Goat Ridge for a while, "then they got real modern and called it Pleasant Hill."

And finally, he said, they hadn't called it anything over the years – "seemed like all the identities have about fizzled out."

Langley also said the local tick problem wasn't nearly as bad as it once was.

However, he said, "you get in them blackberry patches around July and you'll sure get into the chiggers. Them little boogers will eat ya up!"

Cross Bell Ranch (circa 1927) – Trouble in the Osage

The Mullendore Cross Bell Ranch, in the rolling grasslands of the Osage in northeastern Oklahoma, began in the middle 1920s to become one of the largest and illustrious ranches in the state — and, after a mysterious murder 43 years later, among the most legendary in America.

Founded by E.C. "Gene" Mullendore, the ranch, with headquarters in northeast Osage County, near Hulah and west of Copan, grew to cover thousands of acres in parts of both the Sooner State and Kansas. It was once called "Oklahoma's greatest ranching empire."

While some historians place the beginning of the Cross Bell at 1926, published reports say Gene Mullendore acquired the property in 1927 when the ranch, owned by his new father-in-law, Melvin "Buck" Boren, was auctioned in a foreclosure sale.

Gene reportedly made the purchase with the help of his banker-rancher father, Erd C. Mullendore – and Gene and his wife, Kathleen, whom he had married in December 1926, then started the ranch as the Cross Bell.

As to the origin of "Cross Bell," it's believed the name is from the brand used by Gene's grandfather on his mother's side, early-day Oklahoma Territory rancher William Berry – and supposedly had been "an old Mexican mission brand." It was said the Cross Bell brand was on the first Berry cattle that were driven up from Mexico.

For years the Cross Bell Ranch was both a showplace and the icon of a dreamlike West, known for fine cattle grazing on native bluestem, high-bred horses and top cowhands – but it finally began sliding into financial trouble, and its coup de grace came in 1970.

That was when, just before midnight on a Saturday, Sept. 26, Gene's 32-year-old son, E.C. Mullendore III, who had taken over the reins of the ranch some 10 years earlier, was badly beaten and shot between the eyes.

At the time, E.C., whose wife, Linda Vance Mullendore, had left him some six days before and taken their four children and moved out, was at the ranch with his bodyguard, Damon "Chub" Anderson.

Anderson was questioned repeatedly, along with others who had recently visited the ranch, but the queries by authorities failed to net any arrests.

Neither did years of diligent investigating by Sheriff George Wayman and other officers – possibly because of a long delay in the reporting of the crime, and much of the physical evidence had either been lost or destroyed before officers could examine it.

Wayman would say much later that he had "never worked on a case that was any more messed up," and that "we just could never get the evidence we thought it would take to get a conviction."

The ranch went bankrupt two years after the murder. Much of its land and livestock were sold at auction.

Gene Mullendore died the year after that.

The killing of the young cattle baron had instantly exploded into big news throughout the nation. It was reported by media including *The Wall-Street Journal,* and inspired at least one book, "The Mullendore Murder Case," by Jonathan Kwitny.

The incident was called "one of the strangest true stories ever spun out of the West."

And it seemed the murder of E.C. Mullendore would never be solved.

Nearly 80 years after the beginning of the Cross Bell, the place still existed as the home, a model of Western-style comfort and beauty, and the ranch, by that time of approximately 42,000 acres, near tiny Hulah along State Highway 10.

The ranch was being run by Kathleen Mecom Fogarty, granddaughter of Kathleen Mullendore, who had died some years earlier.

Also involved with the ranch was Katsy Mullendore Whittenburg, daughter of the late Gene and Kathleen Mullendore. Katsy, her husband, J.A. "Jim" Whittenburg III, and family were living in Amarillo, Texas, but visited the homestead often.

The ranch's cowboys in recent years had competed, and taken some honors, in the annual Oklahoma Cattlemen's Association Range Round-Up.

Also, the ranch had become known for hosting yearly barbecue events to benefit Elder Care, an organization promoting the wellness and independence of seniors.

And many Oklahomans familiar with the Cross Bell still considered it an impressive and vital part of the state's history and culture.

Frederick F. Drummond, a longtime Osage County rancher from Pawhuska in his middle 70s, called the Cross Bell "still a ranch, with cattle and cowboys" — and with the "big brand" that he said made its front gate truly "elegant."

Ellis Freeny of Edmond, a former rancher in his late 70s who also was a retired manager of the Oklahoma Cattlemen, said he remembered Gene Mullendore as being "very kind to me." And he called the Cross Bell "one of the most popular and famous ranches."

Meanwhile, some new developments in the famous murder case had been reported.

George Wayman, who had retired as sheriff some years earlier and by now was a Fairfax resident in his early 80s, acknowledged that he was re-assigned to the investigation.

And assuming the case had interested present Sheriff Ty Koch, who was shy about communicating with writers, there appeared to be hope that the murder of E.C. Mullendore would finally be solved.

Slapout (1932) – A Small Inventory

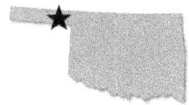

Slapout apparently got its name in 1932 when it began as a store that was a two-room, tarpaper affair along the new State Highway 35 – at that time a graded road — in Beaver County of the Oklahoma Panhandle.

The stories vary, but a popular version has it that the proprietor, the late Tom Lemmons, when asked for something the store didn't have, would often say "We're plumb slap-out of that!"

Also, a written report has it that Lemmons himself once explained that, soon after he opened the small store and gasoline station, it was one of his customers who originated the term.

Lemmons was quoted as saying Fred Jayroe, "one of the road crew," came in to buy something that the store didn't have — "and Fred went back and told the boys . we was just 'slap-out' of that."

And Tom Lemmons thought that would make a fine name.

Close to 75 years after Slapout began, it remained as a tiny community of sorts, including the service station and few other buildings along the highway – which many years before had become the paved State Highway 3, as well as the state's Northwest Passage.

And "Slapout" was both a road sign and the name on the station, which by this time was operated by the High Plains Energy firm.

Frank Lemmons, a retiree in his middle 60s who lived about a mile north, said he had sold the station about five years earlier.

But he said that didn't change what it's called:

"Everybody still knows it by the name of Slapout."

That was especially true throughout the Panhandle, said Dr. V. Pauline Hodges of Beaver, a teacher and official with the No Man's Land Historical Society.

She said she personally found the name meaningful since her father helped build the highway through there "after we lost the farm in the Dust Bowl."

And, she said, "my daddy always laughed at that name, and the man who used to say he was 'slap-out' of everything."

Frank Lemmons said as to exactly how the name came about, "people tell a lot of stories — and they change from day to day."

And he, as much as anyone else, obviously enjoyed them all.

Possum Hollow (circa 1934) – 'A Way of Life'

Possum Hollow is a wooded countryside in Haskell County of eastern Oklahoma that's been called that ever since an unusual incident involving hundreds of the fat and furry mammals.

For many years residents of that rural pocket of the state depended on selling the pelts of opossums ("possums" in local lingo) to supplement their income.

Residents called possum hunting "a way of life." It meant survival.

"That was our bread and butter," once explained John Bates, a local minister and native of the scattered community. He said when he and others were youngsters, "if we had any Christmas in those times, it had to be done with possum hides."

As soon as the weather turned cool, men and boys took their dogs and lanterns and headed for the woods, Bates said.

He once recalled that with one of the best dogs in the community — Ol' Red — "we used to get eighteen to twenty possums with that ol' hound. We'd pile 'em up at a corner fence post and come back with a wagon and team for 'em the next morning."

Another resident who recalled the great possum era was Ruby Davis (It was her late husband, Harmon, who owned Ol' Red).

Ruby also explained how the womenfolk, after the men took the hides for selling, made use of what was left — nothing went to waste. She had one of the best possum recipes in the state.

Possum hunting was such a serious business that at some point over the years, local residents figured out how to get around state game laws, which said the season for possums didn't open until the first of December.

The hunters continued to begin their annual harvest of possums before December, but would pen their catches up until opening day of the season — then would rush their freshly prepared possum hides to market in nearby Keota.

For a month or so, every home in the community had oodles of live possums. Many people kept them in part of a barn, chicken house or other outbuilding. And it was told that one family, whose grown children had left, used a spare bedroom.

That worked well until word got out that a game warden was planning a surprise visit to the community on a certain fall day. He was to arrive at 12 o'clock noon.

So all the residents turned their possums out.

Just before noon that day, John Bates recalled, "possums were all over the community." He said people would be coming down the road in a wagon or horseback, "and see possums – possums were all over the country."

However, no game warden showed up – the alert had been just a rumor. But the whole community, Bates said, "has been called Possum Hollow ever since."

More than 70 years later, Possum Hollow was still a quiet rural community, with its distinctive identity.

Two "Possum Hollow" signs – one along State Highway 9 east of Keota and another farther south on the dirt road – told visitors how to find it. There was also a Possum Hollow church.

And off and on for years, Ruby Davis wrote a column for the *Stigler News-Sentinel* at Stigler, under the heading, "Possum Hollow News."

There still were possums in the woods, too – probably more than ever. Possums weren't hunted there the way they once were, possibly because of changes in the market for furbearer pelts, or the economy in general.

Or maybe the people had changed.

In fact, it was said that a resident once gave directions to a visiting preacher who would be driving there after dark, and added "Be careful and don't run over one of our possums."

Tia Juana (circa 1938) – North of the Border

Tia Juana is an area of scattered homes on the south edge of Grand Lake O' the Cherokees, in Delaware County of northeastern Oklahoma.

It's significant because its name is one of the most unusual in Oklahoma – although the name belies the quiet and overall pleasant ambiance of the small community.

Tia Juana was first called that when it was a gathering of tents and other temporary living quarters for workers who were building the nearby Pensacola Dam – and was also a center for noisy drinking joints and other establishments for male recreation.

Residents over the years have said it once was "a wild little place," with nightspots that catered to "a pretty rough element."

That's when someone, who probably wasn't particular about the spelling, suggested the local place was "almost like Tijuana, Mexico!"

Sometime after the dam was completed in 1940 and the lake was created, the place became a permanent village – mostly of retirees. And although it shed its spicy reputation, it didn't lose its name.

Nearly 70 years after the apparent beginning of Tia Juana, it remained a small place along State Highway 28 a short distance east of Disney, and with a few "Tia Juana" signs here and there.

And it was still both peaceful and respectable, according to Bill Frenchman, who had lived there for nearly 35 years.

However, Frenchman, a 70-year-old former resident of Washington state who was a retired nuclear pipe fitter, was happy to discuss Tia Juana's past.

"You could get anything in Tia Juana, Oklahoma, that you could get in Tijuana, Mexico," he said, adding that when the dam was being built, "that was before penicillin — and there were some things you could get in Tia Juana, Oklahoma, that you couldn't get rid of."

But Frenchman said residents weren't sensitive about Tia Juana's history – well, most of them weren't.

He said once at an informal get-together he heard a local woman remark that she didn't want to see Tia Juana grow, that she wanted to keep it "exactly like it was."

Frenchman said he asked her "Exactly like it was, huh?" Then he named off five onetime local houses of ill repute. "And she turned purple."

Meanwhile, the history of Tia Juana was still occasionally recalled in other towns in that part of the state.

At Disney, Jim Stone, a retired aircraft-manufacturing firm executive who was in his late 60s, didn't wish to elaborate about Tia Juana, but smiled and gave his explanation:

"You might say it was a bedroom community of the Pensacola Dam."

Gene Autry (1941) – A Magic Name

Gene Autry, in Carter County of southern Oklahoma, has been officially called that since Nov. 16, 1941, when an estimated 35,000 folks gathered to honor the local boy who had made good as America's original singing cowboy.

On that day, amid band music and banners and more hoopla than anyone could remember, the man himself was the star attraction and the name of the small town of Berwyn was changed to Gene Autry.

The post office made it official the next Jan. 1, and all of Oklahoma was proud – except for Autry's real hometown about 15 miles away.

And all this despite the fact that Autry apparently forgot the state, including the town of Gene Autry.

Autry was born in Texas, but grew up at Ravia, in Johnston County, where his family moved when he was small.

After he became famous as a top Hollywood star and recording

artist, he established his Flying A Ranch, a rodeo stock contracting operation, near Berwyn. It was then decided that he would adopt Berwyn, as "Gene Autry."

Autry, known for Western movies and such songs as "Back in the Saddle Again" and "Rudolph the Red-Nosed Reindeer," built a multi-million-dollar fortune in broadcasting and became the original owner of the California Angels baseball team.

After the big ceremony in 1941, Autry never permanently returned to Oklahoma.

For several years, Bobby Newton, a local rancher and president of the local chamber of commerce, worked hard to promote his town as Autry's namesake, declaring "the magic of 'Gene Autry' is all we've got going for us."

But Autry's headquarters in California didn't share his passion. That was about the time Autry was establishing his own $54 million Gene Autry Museum of Western Heritage in Los Angeles.

In 1990, local people established the Gene Autry Oklahoma Museum, an admission-free exhibit housed in a former schoolhouse. They also began an annual, four-day Gene Autry Oklahoma Film and Music Festival, to be held every Sept. 29, Gene's birthday.

Meanwhile, residents of Ravia indicated they had never been highly entertained by the celebrated singing cowboy.

Louella Oglesby, a retired Ravia teacher who knew Gene Autry before he left home and found stardom, said Autry "wasn't a hero as far as we're concerned – he didn't do a thing for Ravia."

At Marietta, one of Gene Autry's kinfolks, Mel Autry — who happened to be a real, off-the-screen cowboy — passed along a few memories about his third cousin.

Mel recalled being tired of hearing Gene "pick that ol' guitar," while he himself was never musical – "I can hardly play a jukebox."

Also, Mel, a retired working cowhand and former professional rodeo contender, said the two of them weren't especially close, and once they were both at the same rodeo — Gene as the featured entertainer and Mel as a rough stock rider.

Mel said at first they only exchanged a nod – but then he made an impressive ride on two bad broncs, and he was acknowledged by his more famous relative.

"After that," Mel said, "he was just puddin' and pie."

Some 65 years after the town of Gene Autry was named, the town was still a place of about 100 people.

Gene Autry, at age 91, had died about eight years earlier.

Both the local Autry museum and the Autry music festival brought in some 15,000 visitors a year, according to Elvin Sweeten, a retired teacher in his middle 60s who managed both with the help of his wife, Flo.

He said the museum, while financed locally, had received some of Gene's personal items from the Autry center in California, along with some moral support – "they started talkin' to us."

Bobby Newton, in his middle 60s and still the head of the local chamber, suggested the local museum was more representative of Gene Autry himself than the much larger and grander Autry museum "way out there in California."

Besides, he said, "this one is free!"

At nearby Ravia, longtime resident Louella Oglesby still held that the renaming of Berwyn to honor Gene Autry in 1941 "didn't amount to a hill of beans."

And at Marietta, Mel Autry, in his late 70s and still considered a cowboy, repeated what he had said years before about the town of Gene Autry:

"I still call it Berwyn."

Red Rock Canyon (1956) – Unique, Sorta

Red Rock Canyon, a name that conjures up scenes of beauty and adventure, describes one of Oklahoma's most interesting land formations – even if the name doesn't belong exclusively to Oklahoma.

As a steep canyon in a region of red sandstone and a variety of trees in Caddo County a short distance west of the center of the state, it's known as Red Rock Canyon State Park.

But it's not the only Red Rock Canyon. It's reported there are places with that same name in perhaps 30 other states.

The canyon in Oklahoma apparently was given the name of Red Rock when it was established as a state park in 1956, park officials say. Before that it had been known as Kiwanis Camp Park since the 1930s.

Much earlier, historians believe, the canyon was a winter camp for Plains Indians. And it apparently was a camping place for gold seekers heading west on the California Road in the late 1840s and early 1850s, when the area was part of what was then the Choctaw and Chickasaw lands of Indian Territory.

But among modern folks, it's better known as a place of recreation, ranging from quiet picnicking to rappelling – some 80 feet down its sheerest wall. In other parts of the canyon, it's about 150 feet from the top to the bottom.

And regardless of how many other "Red Rock Canyons" there are, Oklahomans seem to like theirs.

Fifty years after the state's Red Rock Canyon apparently got its name, the park continued to host a bunch of visitors, according to manager David Sutton.

"It's a very popular name," he said, acknowledging the large number of places in other states with the same designation.

However, the canyon in Oklahoma, with its some 25 varieties of trees and its soft red canyon walls, had been called unique enough. Besides, state residents enjoyed the place for various reasons. Lillie Cox of Hinton said she visited the canyon daily before going to work as a clerk at the nearby Cherokee Trading Post on Interstate 40.

"I walk down there every morning," she said, noting that some recent area improvements had improved it. "It's beautiful, and a perfect place to walk – out of the wind, with lots of shade. And it's just like it always was – except the roads are better."

Lottawatta Road (circa 1964) – A Way of Talkin'

Lottawatta Road is probably best known as a name for an exit on I-40 where it crosses a portion of Lake Eufaula in McIntosh County of eastern Oklahoma.

The road, which has come to be considered a scattered community, is believed to have been named in 1964 when what was then the Oklahoma State Department of Highways was completing that exit on I-40. The interstate was still being built, the section in that area being completed in the early 1970s, and fully completed in 1975.

For several years, travelers who would see the "Lottawatta" sign – including many Oklahomans – assumed the name was an Indian word.

But the origin of the name was finally revealed — and as one of the simplest in the state.

It was reported that Don Garrett, who was on the highway department's road drafting squad that was planning exit signs, came up with it as a temporary name – but the workers around him liked it, so it became permanent.

More than three decades after the marker was put up, questions and comments about it finally resulted in an explanation in *The Daily Oklahoman* by columnist Robert E. Lee.

In his column on Nov. 18, 1998, Robert explained it after hearing about it from a reader, and it was further confirmed by state officials.

It was said that when Garrett's crew inspected the road, he saw that it "didn't go much of anywhere except down to the water," and that "Don just thought up that name and wrote it on the map, thinking someone would find a more proper name before signs were made and installed."

Garrett was also quoted as saying the road had "a lot of water" – only the informal way he said it, it came out "a lotta water."

So, according to state transportation department officials, Garrett's fellow workers right then agreed on "Lottawatta" – combining what some of them called an Indian spelling with "his Okie accent."

More than 40 years after Lottawatta Road was named, the area, a short drive west of Checotah, was comprised of a convenience store called Fort Lottawatta, another business called Staveley Storage and a few homes.

At the Fort Lottawatta store, Carol Stafford, who managed the business along with her husband, Cal, a man in his late 40s, and her sister, Dena Peacock, was fond of discussing the name – and passing along information about it.

And that's why their store was called that, she said. "I liked the name Lottawatta, and my husband wanted to put 'Fort' in front of it."

Carol, originally from California, also said she had wanted a name for their business that "sounded like Oklahoma."

And when she saw "Lottawatta" on the highway sign, she knew she had found it.

Nowhere (circa 1976) – Definitely There

Nowhere, a small store amid a cluster of homes near the south end of Fort Cobb Lake in Caddo County, apparently got its name in the middle 1970s when a new owner made a less-than-enthusiastic remark about the location.

It's said that a family who had lived in California bought the business site, and the husband decided to name it after something his wife said.

About 30 years after Nowhere began, it was still a store, and the name had attached itself to the surrounding tiny community as well. Also, it was regularly mentioned by news people, as a check station during hunting seasons, and occasionally by people when giving directions as a point of location in the southwestern quarter of the state.

Jerry Howell, a man in his late 50s who had owned the store for more than 25 years, had grown accustomed to answering questions about the name – and hearing plenty of funny comments about it.

He said the business, which previously was known as Ben's Boat House, acquired its present name when it was bought by the Milo Carl family – and when Milo's wife, Lydia Belle, gave her evaluation of the place.

"And the story I got," Howell explained, "they were from California, and there's lots of people out there – and his wife thought this place was terrible. And she said 'We're out in the middle of nowhere!'"

So Jerry, who bought the business about three years later, decided it would be hard to improve on a name like that.

"People get a kick out of it – people from all over," he said. "I hear things like 'You're not here, you're nowhere!,' and all kinds of jokes about it."

And the publicity, he said, hasn't hurt his business. "I'm pretty lucky about that."

Also, in that portion of the state, it's easy for people to find. For instance, if you're in the nearby town of Fort Cobb, all you have to do is ask anyone "Where's Nowhere?"

Besides, as the crow flies, it's only about 20 miles northeast of another one of Oklahoma's well-known landmarks. It's a place called Dirty Shame.

Afterword

It's been said that every nice memory becomes an ineffably beautiful picture when one looks back at it through the distance of years. That could describe one of many strong feelings that seize us as we're swept along by this mysterious but powerful current we call Time.

With the preceding words on places, I have tried to transcend, and join others of my homeland in looking back through a century of statehood and more.

Such a view reveals people's struggles, misdeeds and sadness, but also a few of their moments of joy and laughter. Their journey through Time has been brief, and bumpy, but sometimes fun.

I hope all Oklahomans feel as I do, that it's worth remembering.

The Author

Index

A

"A Tour on the Prairies," 24
Abernathy, Bud, 144
Abernathy, Jack "Catch 'em Alive," 144
Abernathy, Temple, 144
Abilene, Kansas, 49, 50
Acre, W.H., 16
Ada, 91, 92, 145
Adair County, 19, 32, 73, 149, 183, 198
Adair County Historical Society, 183
Adams, Elaine, 35
Adams, Frieda Jo Ann, 148
Adm. Richard Byrd, 55
Afton, 67, 68
Agent John D. Miles, 63
Ah-daw-ate, 20
Aitson, Rev. Lucius, 120
Alaska, 104
Albert, Carl, 167
Albuquerque, New Mexico, 71
Alcorn, Grandville, 109
Alcorn, Robert, 109
"All My Friends Are Hookers," 161
Allen, Harold, 105, 106
Allen, Joe, 92
Allen, Yvonne, 106
Altus, 18, 66
Alverson, Harold, 77
Amarillo, Texas, 36, 201
America, 54, 104, 161, 165, 166, 200, 209
"America, Oklahoma," 166
American, 55, 62, 123, 170
American Indian, 1, 2, 85, 123
American Legion, 160
American West, 123
Americana, 125
Anadarko, x, 20
Anderson, Damon "Chub," 201
Anderson, Ronnie, 31
Anderson, W.K. "Bill," 167

"Annie Get Your Gun," 107
Annie Oakley, 107
Antelope Hills, 34, 35, 36
Anti-Horsethief Association, 114
Apache, 63, 123, 145, 197
Appalachians, 22
Arbuckle Mountains, 132
Arapaho, 48, 63, 95
Archer, Earl, 181
Argo, Jim, x
Arizona, 20, 123
Arkansas, 22, 49, 97, 193
Arkansas River, 8, 10, 23, 24, 25, 40, 82
"Arkansas Tom" Jones, 53
Army, 31, 34, 44, 45, 49, 119, 135, 147, 166
Army Corps of Engineers, 11
Arnett, 38, 110
Asher, 71
Askew, Melvin, 119
Atoka, 31
Atoka County, 30, 107
Atoka Lake, 108
Autry, Gene, 209, 210, 211
Autry, Mel, 210, 211
Awa'hili, 73

B

B County, 126
Babbs Switch, 187-189
Babbs Switch School, 188
Babcock, 187
Baby Doll, 151
Bachmann, Calvin, 36
"Back in the Saddle Again," 210
Baker, George Leon, 166
Bales, Kenneth, 131
"Ballad of the Fairmount Cowboy, The," 102
Bandera, Texas, 66
"Bandit Queen, The," 74, 77

Banner, H.T., 180
Barber, Wayne, 190
Bar-O-Bar, 58
Barnes, Lee Ann, 118
Barton, John Yudell, 65, 66
Bates, John, 205, 206
Battle of Honey Springs, 151
Battle of Middle Boggy, 30
Battle of the Washita, 34
Beaver, 9, 203
Beaver County, 9, 87, 203
"Beck faction," 32
Beckham County, 4, 156, 158
Beer City, 87, 88
Beers, William, 133
Bell, Curtis, 84
"Belle Starr's ghost," 77
Ben's Boat House, 216
Berlin, 136, 137
Bernice, 67, 68
Berry, William, 200
Berwyn, 209, 210, 211
Bickford, 155
Bielich, Peggy, 83
Big Boggy, 30
Big Pasture, 143, 145
Big Pasture News, 144
Big Pasture School, 144, 145
Big Tree, 20
Biggers, Lillie, 188
Biggers, Margaret, 188
Biggers, Walter, 188
Biggers, William, 188
Bishop, Diane, 41
"Bill" Anderson, 167
"Bitter Creek" Newcomb, 53
Bitting Springs, 73
Black Beaver, 48, 49
Black Hills, 19
"Black Kettle Lake," 80, 81
Black Kettle Museum, 81
Black Kettle National Grassland, 34, 80
"Black Kettle Recreation Area," 81
Black Mesa, 8, 44, 45
Black Mesa Bed and Breakfast, 45
Blackburn, Bob, *x*
Blaine County, 48, 117, 154
Blake, Betty, 104

Blake, William "Tulsa Jack," 53
Blankenship, Sheila, 161
Blevins, Viola, 43
"Blind Mack," 152
"Bob" Klemme, 50
Bobbitt, A.A. "Gus," 92
Boggy Creek, 30
Boggy Depot, 30
Boggy Depot State Park, 31
Bointy, Jack, 20
Boise City, 9
Bolding, Dow, 187
Bond, Kaye, *x*
Bonnie & Clyde Tamaha General Store, 41
"Boom Town," 191
Boot Hill, 168
"Bootlegger," 91
Boren, Melvin "Buck," 200
Borrero, "Mexican Joe," 56
"Boundary Mountains," 34
Bowlegs, 134, 135
Bowlegs, Billy, 134
Box, 176
Boyen-tday, 20
Bradford, Susan Cabaniss, 5
Bradshaw-Packsaddle Bridge, 38
Bradshaw, State Rep. Mark "Buzz," 38
Brankel, Charles, 186
Brannon, Denise, 167
Brannon, Gaylon, 167
Braun, Lillie, 188
Braun, Matt, 187
Break O'Day Farm and Metcalfe Museum, 35
Briggs, Frank, 53
Briscoe, Dan J., 66
British, 59
Broadway, 107
"Broncos," 131
Brother Dominic Lambert, 71
Brown, Father Matthew, 71
Brownsville, Texas, 50, 180
Brozek, Jean Bartlett, 102
Bryan, William Jennings, 55
Bryce, Delf A. "Jelly," 120
Buchanan, Kelley, 135
"Buck" Boren, 200

"Buck" Nall, 112
"Buckskin Joe" Works, 16
Buffalo, 186
Buffalo Creek, 185
"Buffalo Creek Chronicles," 186
Bugtussle, 167
Bugtussle School, 167
Bunch, Gove, 68
Burbank Oil Field, 191
Burch, Jim, 86
Burge, David, 97, 98
"BUR-len," 136
Burleson, Texas, 135
Burnett, Burk, 144
Burney, Pete, 138, 139
Burney, Ruby, 139
Burrell, Berry, 92
Butterfield Overland Stage Line, 30
"Buzz" Bradshaw, 38
Buzzards' Roost, 115, 116
Byars, 49
Byrd, Adm. Richard, 55
Byington, Cyrus, 26

C

Caddo, 2, 14
Caddo County, 46, 115, 195, 196, 212, 216
Caldwell, Kansas, 50, 61
California, 34, 56, 81, 97, 152, 168, 169, 196, 211, 215, 216
California Angels, 210
California Road, 34, 130, 212
California Station, 89
Calisay, 20
Calloway, Thomas, 63
Camargo, 69, 70, 110
"Camp Ferdinandina," 11
Camp Napoleon, 42
Camp Tom Hale, 74
Campbell, K.D. "Chubb," 136
Campbell, Nelona, 136
Campbell, Winston, 94
Canada, 19
Canadian County, 95, 130
Canadian River, 34, 37, 69, 90, 91, 110, 130, 190

Cañón del Diablo, 4
Caney, 31
Capitol (U.S.), 22
Captain A.S. Mangum, 83
"Captain Bill Coe," 44
Captain Billy's Whiz Bang, 191
Carey, Roy "Pee Wee," 99
Carl, Lydia Belle, 216
Carl, Milo, 216
Carlos, 20
Carnegie, 195
Carrizo Creek, 8, 44
Carter County, 182, 209
Carter's Station, 195
Casey, Jean Ann, 64
"Cat," 138
"Catch 'em Alive" Abernathy, 144
Catholic faith, 71
Cave Springs, 74
"Celebrate the Western Trail," 66
Cement, 115, 116
Cement Museum and Jesse James Visitors' Center, 115
Centennial Celebration, 50, 161
Centennial Celebration of the 101, 56
"Centennial Dempsey School," 163
Chance, 198
Checotah, 153, 215
Cherokee, 14, 22, 23, 24, 29, 32, 48, 49, 73, 103, 117, 149, 174, 177
Cherokee Advocate, The, 149
Cherokee Council, 32
Cherokee County, 23, 32, 121, 149
Cherokee Heritage Center, 23
"Cherokee Kid, The," 104
Cherokee Nation, 22, 23, 24, 32, 33, 67, 73, 82, 89, 103, 121, 128, 149, 168, 174, 176
Cherokee National Capitol, 23
Cherokee National Council, 32
Cherokee National Holiday, 23
Cherokee Outlet, 55
Cherokee Strip, 59, 61, 125
"Cherokee Strip," 55
Cherokee Strip Cow Punchers Association, 57
Cherokee Strip Museum, *x*
Cherokee Trading Post, 213

Cherokee Trail of Tears Association, 33
Cheyenne, 38, 63, 81, 95, 117, 136, 181
Cheyenne and Arapaho lands, 35, 48, 69, 80, 95, 109, 117, 136, 154
Cheyenne-Arapaho, 63
Chicago, 176
Chicago, Rock Island and Pacific Railroad, 146
Chickasaw, 14
Chickasaw Nation, 30, 93, 99, 130, 132
Chickasaw National Recreation Area, 132
Chickie, 107
Chickiechokie, 107
Chief Black Kettle, 34
Chief Going Snake, 33
Chief Left Hand, 48
Chief Lone Wolf, 19
Chief Peta Nocona, 16
Chief Santana, 119
Chief White Eagle, 57
Chisholm, Jesse, 48, 49, 50
Chisholm Springs, 49
Chisholm Trail, 48, 49, 50, 51, 61, 62, 65, 66
Chisholm Trail Heritage Center, 50, 51
Chisholm Trail Historical Museum, 50
Chisholm Trail Museum, 50
Chisholm, William, 50
Chism, 50
"Choc" beer, 152
Chockie, 107
Choctaw, 14, 24, 26, 27, 30, 40, 42, 76, 174
Choctaw County, 140
Choctaw and Chickasaw lands, 212
"Choctaw Definer," 26
Choctaw Nation, 2, 26, 30, 40, 76, 107, 140, 165, 167
Christie, 198
Christie, Ned, 73
Christmas, 187, 202
Christmas Eve, 187, 189
"Chub" Anderson, 201
"Chubb" Campbell, 136
Church of the Sacred Heart and the Immaculate Conception, 71
Cimarron, 8, 9

Cimarron Bait N' Tackle, 9
Cimarron Boulevard, 9
Cimarron City, 9
Cimarron County, 9, 44
Cimarron River, 7, 52, 59, 113, 186
Cimarron Road, 9
"Cimarron Territory," 9
Cimarron Territory Celebration, 9
Cimarron Trail, 9
"Cimarron," 8
"City of Springs, The," 132
Civil Service, 144
Civil War, 30, 40, 42, 82, 115, 151, 152
Claremore, 76, 104
Clarksville, Texas, 57
Clay, Henry, 57
Clear Boggy Creek, 30, 31
Clear Creek Lake, 99
Cleo Springs, 60
Clifton, Dan "Dynamite Dick," 53
Clothier, A.C., 185
Clowers, Willie Mae, 165
Coe, Bill, 44, 45
Coe, Cyrus, 44
Coe, William, 44
Coffey, Gene, 25
Coffey, Jim, 159
Coffey, Nancy, 25
Col. George Washington Miller, 55, 58
Coleman, I.Z., 183
Colorado, 97, 162
Colorado Territory, 44, 45
Colson, Debbie, 87
"Colt Corral, the," 88
Comanche, 5, 14, 15, 16, 17, 18, 19, 20, 34, 37, 63, 104, 115, 119, 144, 145, 197
Comanche County, 28, 123
Comanche, Kiowa and Apache lands, 15, 16, 19, 42, 115, 119, 123, 141, 143, 146
Comanche, Kiowa and Apache Agency, 63
Comancheros, 36
Combs, Ben, 152
Combs, Benny, 151
Combs, Willard, 151, 152

"Come Tour with Me – Tales of the Big Pasture," 145
Commerce, 105
Community Museum, 10
Confederate, 30, 40, 41, 55, 115, 152
Conley, Robert J., 33
Conners, Bill, 91
Cook, Alva "Dobber," 142
Cook, Connie, 67
Cook, Ed, 63
"Cook gang," 23
Cooper, John, 58
Cooperton, 28
Copan, 200
Copeland, Roger, 135
Cornelsen, Bill, 60
Corner, 91, 92, 126
Corner Saloon, 92
Cornett, Henry, 58
Coronado, 36
Corps of Engineers, 11
Corpus Christi, Texas, 56
"Colt Corral, the," 88
Cotton County, 144
Council Grove, 48
County F, 136
Courtney, Lonnie, 172
Cowboy Hill, 54, 57
Cox, Eldon, 125
Cox, Lillie, 213
Cox, Lizzie, 125
Cox, Merle, 75
Cozy Corner, 152
"Cradle of Oklahoma Catholicism, the," 71
Crane, Glena Belle, 81
Craig, James, 70
Craig, Lee, 70
Crawford, 80
Crawford, Isabel, 120
Crawford, Robert Wade, 111
Crawford School, 111
Crawford, Tom, 136
"Crazy Horse," 149
Creek, 14, 78
Creek Nation, 78, 111, 138, 151
Critser, Claudia, 161

Croppy, 58
Cross Bell, 200, 201, 202
"Cross Bell," 200
Cross Bell Ranch, 200
Cruce, Mrs. Lee, 107
"Curbstone Kirby" Smedley, 57
Curtis, Marilyn Smith, 182
Custer, Lt. Col. George A., 34, 38
Cutthroat Gap, 28

D

Daily Oklahoman, The, x, 95, 214
Dale, Edward Everett, 16
Dale, H.P., 16
Dalton, Bill, 53
"Dances with Wolves," 149
Daniels' Spring, 178
"Dark Cloud," 103
Darlington, 63
Darrigrand, S.A. "Tom," 56
Daugherty, Roy, 53
Davis, Clara, 163
Davis, Harmon, 205
Davis, Leon, 163
Davis, Lester, 163
Davis, Linda, 163
Davis, Ruby, 205, 206
Day County, 109
de Galvez, Bernardo, 12
"Deacon Jim" Miller, 92
Dead Indian Lake, 80
Dead Indian Creek, 80, 81
"Dead Indian Creek," 81
"Dead Indian Lake," 80, 81
Dean, Dizzy, 190, 191
Dean, Jay Hanna, 190
Dean, Jerome Herman, 190
Dean, Michael, x
Dean, Monroe, 193
Deer Creek, 10
"Deer Creek Site, the," 11
DeFrange, Ann, 95
Delaware, 48, 89
Delaware County, 67, 128, 207
Delaware County Genealogical Society, 67

Delaware Indian, 48, 89
DeLonais, Francis, 72
DeLonais, James, 72
DeLonais, Norma, 72
Delvan, Dorothy Whitehorse, 28
Deming, New Mexico, 97
Democratic Convention, 145
Dempsey, 162, 163, 164
Dempsey, Jack, 56, 162
Dennis, Mildred, 172
Denoya, 191, 192
Department of Agriculture, 125
Department of Transportation, 59
Department of Wildlife Conservation, 35
"Depot on the Boggy, the," 30
Devil's Canyon, 4, 5
Devol, 144
Dewey County, 69
DeWitt, Donald, x
"Diablo," 5
Dick, Bart, 183
Dickson, George, 73
Dickson, Levi, 73
Dickson, Loretta, 73
Dickson, Thomas, 186
Dirty Shame, 195, 196, 197, 217
"Dirty Shame Gourd Club," 197
"Dirty Shame Lady," 196
"Dirty Shame, OK," 196
Disney, 207, 208
Dizzy Dean Day, 193, 194
Doan, C.F., 65
Doan's Crossing, 65, 66
"Dobber" Cook, 142
Dobbs, Jerry, 23
Dodge City, Kansas, 87
Dodge City Trail, 65
Dog Iron Ranch, 104
Dogtown, 111, 112
"Dogtown Bottom," 111, 112
Doolin, Bill, 52, 53
Dorothy, 163
Doxey, 136
Dr. Bob Wyatt, 145
Dr. Charlie Ogle, 50
Dr. Chris Jefferies, 51
Dr. Clyde Snow, 169

Dr. Lewis Stiles, 26
Dr. Terry J. Schreiner, 112
Dr. V. Pauline Hodges, 203
Dragoons, 4
Dragoon expedition, 4
Drennan, Lura, 152
Drummond, Frederick F., 202
Dry Cimarron River, 8
Duck, Kevin, 170, 171
Duke, 5
Duncan, 50, 51, 99, 112, 182
Dunn, John, 37
Dunn John Jr., 37
Durgan, Millie, 20
Durham, 35, 36
Dust Bowl, 1, 204
Dustin, 111
Dye, Karen, 10, 11
"Dynamite Dick" Clifton, 53

E

Eagle Town, 26
Eagletown, 26, 27
East, 89
East Central University, 145
Eastern Cherokees, 22, 32
Eaton, Frank "Pistol Pete," 113
Eck, Kenneth, 182
Edmond, 154, 202
Edwards, Whit, x
Ehler, Annette B., 63
El Dorado, 97
El Potrero, 88
Elder Care, 201
"Elder-AIDA," 97
Eldorado, 97
Elephant Saloon, 87
Elgin, 20
Elk City, 158
Ellis County, 34, 37, 109
English, 4, 20, 143, 190, 145, 170, 193
English-Choctaw, 26
Enid, x, 50
Europe, 94
Evans, Jean Webb, 58
Evatt, Dessie, 120

F

Fairchild, Emery, 110
Fairfax, 202
Fairless, Willie Mae, 166
Fairmount Cemetery, 101
"Fairmount Cowboy 1890, The," 102
Fairview, 60
Falkner, Jim, 82
Falkner, Virginia, 82
Fant, George, 63
Farris, Bob, 88
Farris Well Service, 88
Father Isidore Robot, 71
Father Matthew Brown, 71
Federal Aviation Administration, 131, 163
Federal Communications Commission, 193
Fegel, Leojenne, 70
Ferber, Edna, 8
Ferdinand, King, 10
"Ferdinand the Bull," 11
Ferdinandina, 10
"Fernando Point," 11
Fields, Marlene, 192
Fine, Cathy, 174
Finley, 178, 179
1st Kansas Infantry (Colored), 152
First Lady of Oklahoma, 107
Fitz, Dord, 36
Five Civilized Tribes, 14, 22, 23
Flint Ridge, 129
Flowery Mound, 167
Flying A Ranch, 207
Fogarty, Kathleen Mecom, 201
Folsum, New Mexico, 45
Fondren, Margie, 93
Forehand, Judy, 83
Fort Cobb, 217
Fort Cobb Lake, 216
"Fort Fernadina," 11
Fort Gibson, 4, 25
Fort Lottawatta, 215
Fort Lyon, 45
Fort Nichols, 44, 45
"Fort Prentice," 40, 41
Fort Sill, x, 61, 63, 123, 124
Fort Smith, Arkansas, 74
Fort Union, 45
Fort Worth, Texas, 135
Foster, Gene, 75
Fourteen Mile Creek, 122
France, 10, 12
Frankford, Hattie, 162
Frankford, Web, 162
Franklin, John Hope, 151
Franklin, Wirt, 182
Freeny, Ellis, 202
French, 10, 30, 72
French Benedictine, 71
Frenchman, Bill, 207, 208
Frenchmen, 12
Frisco Railroad, 187
Frogville, 140
Frost, Charles, 140
Fuchs, Y.C., 158
Furr, T. Wayne, x

G

Gable, Clark, 191
Gable, Will, 191
Gantz, George, 36
Gardner, Frances, 169
Gardner, Jefferson, 26
Gardner Mansion, 26
Garrett, Don, 214
Gass, Florene, 184
Gates, Jim, 57
Gen. Don Diego Ortiz Parrilla, 12
Gen. Henry Leavenworth, 49
Gen. John J. Pershing, 55
Gene Autry, 209, 210, 211
Gene Autry Museum of Western Heritage, 210
Gene Autry Oklahoma Film and Music Festival, 210
Gene Autry Oklahoma Museum, 210
"Gene" Mullendore, 200
Georgia, 67, 89
German, 95, 137
Germany, 136, 196
Geronimo, 123, 124
"Geronimo: An American Legend," 149
Geronimo Birthday Celebration, 124

Ghost Hollow, 52, 53
Ghost Mound, 46, 47
Gibson, Hoot, 56
Girdner, O.T. "Pete," 180
Gist, Harold, 2, 3
Gladys' Beer and Cigarette Outlet, 88
Glass Mountains, 59, 60
Gloss Mountain Conservancy, Inc., 60
Gloss Mountain State Park, 60
"Gloss Mountains," 60
Gloss Mountains Cruisers' Car Show, 60
Goat Ridge, 198
God, 102
Going Snake, 32, 33
Goingsnake, 32, 33
Goingsnake Creek, 32
Goingsnake District Heritage Association, 32
Goingsnake Historical District Association, 32
Goingsnake Historical Society, 32
"Goingsnake Massacre, the," 32
Goingsnake Messenger, The," 32, 33
Goins, Charles R., *x*
Gold Bells Mine, 141
Golda's Mill, 73
Golda's Old Stone Milling Co., 73
Gonzales, Alecia, *x*
Goodnight, Sue, 172, 173
Goodwell, *x*, 87
Goombi, J.T., 20
Gore, 176, 177
Gotebo, 146, 147, 148
Gotebo Get Down, 147
Gotebo News, 148
Gov. Frank Keating, 150
Grace Community Church, 170
Grady County, 42
Grand, 109, 110
Grand Lake O' the Cherokees, 67, 207
Grand Ole Opry, 107
Grand River, 24, 67
Grandfield, 144, 145
"Grandpa Thorpe," 85
Grant County, 61
Grayson, 138, 139
Great Depression, 1

Great Plains National Bank, 97
"Great Spanish Road to Red River," 5
Great State of Sequoyah Commission, 23
Great Western Performers, 107
Great Western Trail, 37, 65, 66, 69
"Great Western Trail Museum," 66
Green, Bob, 165
Green, Ron, 50
"Green Grow the Lilacs," 76
Greenfield, 48
Greer County, 4
Greer County, Texas, 4, 16, 65, 83
Gregory, Cyndy, 124
Greife, Sherry, 104
Griggs, Allan, 45
Grimes, 159
Grove, 67
Guess, George, 22
"Gus" Bobbitt, 92
Guthrie, 56, 168, 169
Guthrie, Glenita, 33
Gypsum Hills, 117

H

Haley, Jack, 28, 29
Hall of Fame (Baseball), 190
Hamleton, Mary, 20
Hamilton, Gladys, 57
Haney, Mary, 64
"Hanging Judge" Parker, 74
Hardcastle, Stoney, 112
Harding, Warren G., 55
Harmon County, 4, 101
Harper County, 185
Harris, Cyrus, 30
Harris, Phil, x
Harrison, Betty, 60
"Harry Leslie," 110
Hartley, Charlie, 36
Hartley, June, 36
Haskell County, 40, 76, 205
Haskell County Historical Society, 77
"Hat Made of Ermine Pelt," 146
"Haunted Canyon," 5
Hays, Mark, 99
Healdton, 182

Healdton Herald, 182
Healdton-Hewitt Oil Field, 182
Hearst, William Randolph, 56
Hebensperger, Jim, 188
Hebensperger, Joe, 188
Heirholzer, Joseph, 186
Heisch, Melvina Thurman, 35
Hennessey, 50, 62, 64
"Hennessy Massacre," 62
Hennessy, Pat, 62, 63, 64
"Hennesy," 62
Hennis, Gary, 53
Henryetta, 111
Hensley, Norma Jean, 67, 68
Heritage Center, 10
Hess, 65
"Hidalgo," 179
High Plains Energy, 203
Highfill, Bennett, 186
Hightower, Leon, 155
Hill, Bob, 153
Hill, Sam, 57
Hillerman, Tony, 71, 72, 149
Hinton, 210
"Historical Atlas of Oklahoma," *x*
Historical Preservation Committee, 144
Hitchin' Post, 36
Hobart, 16, 19, 187, 188, 189
Hobart Cemetery, 188
Hodges, Dr. V. Pauline, 203
Hoffman, 138, 139
Hoig, Stan, 49
Hokanson, Sue, 6
Holder, Ben, 113
Holder, Teresa, 113
Hollis, 101
Holloway, Rex, 110
Hollywood, 16, 103, 149, 191, 209
Holman, Betty, 174
Holman, Bill, 174
Holman, Dale, 174
Holman, Hubert, 174
Home of Sequoyah, 22, 23
"Home of the World's Oldest Rattlesnake Hunt," 117
Honey Springs Battlefield Park, 152
Hooker, 160, 161
Hooker Advance, The, 161

Hooker Chamber of Commerce, 161
"Hooker Horny Toads," 160, 161
"Hooker School," 161
"Hooker Street Walk," 161
Hooker Threldkeld, 161
"Hooker" Threldkeld, 160
Hope, 99
Hope, Bob, 104
Hope Community Church, 99
Horan, Henry, 57
Horsethief Canyon, 113, 114
Houston, Sam, 24, 49, 109
Houston, Sequoyah, 23
Houston, Temple, 109
Howard, A.L., 18
Howard McCasland Field House, 99
Howard, Sam C., 18
Howell, Gary Ray, *x*
Howell, Jerry, 216
Hudspeth, Debbie, 41
Hueston, Tom, 53
Hughes County, 78, 193
Hughes County Times, The, 79
Hulah, 200, 201
Hungarian, 56
Hunting Horse, 119
Hyder, Glenn, 77
Hydro, 46

I

I-40, 214
Idabel, 166
Illinois, 97
Illinois River, 177
Indian, 2, 4, 5, 10, 12, 13, 14, 15, 16, 17, 18, 20, 22, 29, 34, 37, 40, 42, 44, 46, 48, 49, 52, 55, 56, 63, 72, 76, 80, 81, 89, 95, 96, 103, 105, 116, 119, 123, 124, 126, 143, 144, 145, 146, 152, 154, 158, 174, 197, 214

Indian Mission Cemetery, 120
Indian Nation Turnpike, 111
"Indian Nations," 23
Indian Removal Act, 14

Indian Territory, 2, 4, 14, 15, 16, 19, 22, 23, 24, 26, 28, 30, 32,34, 37, 40, 42, 46, 48, 49, 52, 54, 59, 61, 62, 63, 67, 69, 71, 73, 74, 76, 78, 80, 82, 85, 89, 91, 93, 99, 103, 105, 107, 111, 121, 126, 128, 130, 132, 134, 138, 140, 149, 151, 154, 165, 167, 170, 174, 176, 212
"Indian Territory," 2
Ingalls, 52, 53
Ingalls Shoot-Out Re-enactment, 53
Inman, Jeannie, 89, 90
In-na-tah-oolo-sah, 32
Internet, 161
Interstate 40, 213
Iowa, 97
Iowa Indian lands, 113
Ireland, 62
Irving, Washington, 24
"It's Gonna Be OK – A Lease Child's Legacy," 172

J

"J.J. Hill," 115
J.O. Jones General Store, 128, 129
J.R. Williams, 40, 41
Jackson County, 4, 15, 65, 97
Jackson, Dennis, 177
James, Frank, 115
James, Jesse, 115
January, Max, 90
Jayroe, Fred, 203
Jefferies, Dr. Chris, 51
Jefferson, 50
Jefferson County, 12
"Jelly" Bryce, 120
"Jesse Chisholm's Grave,"
"Jim" Whittenburg III, 201
Johannesmeyer, Paul, 118
Johnson, Ben, 104
Johnson, Joe, 105
Johnson, Larry, 140
Johnson, Mickey, 127
Johnson, Omie, 140
Johnson, Robert Grady, 124
Johnson, Sam, 172
Johnston County, 209

Johnston, Harry Wayne, 11
Jones, "Arkansas Tom,"
Jones, Bill, 121, 122
Jones, Buck, 56
Jones, Gilbert, 178, 179
Jones, Harry, 69
Jones, Henry C., 85
Jones, Jim, 135
Jones, Nancy, 122
Jones, Sue, 18
Jordan, Larry, 90
Julian, Becky, 131

K

Kansas, 8, 48, 49, 50, 58, 65, 66, 87, 88, 97, 128, 129, 151, 162, 200
Kansas City, 128
Kansas City, Kansas, 128
Kansas City, Missouri, 128
Katy Railroad, 69
Kauley, Ernestine Kauahquo, 19
Kaw Lake, 10, 11
Kay County, 10, 57
Keahey, Leona, 80, 81
Keating, Gov. Frank, 150
Kemp, Buddy, 57
Kemp, Tom, 145
Kennedy, Arthur, 171
Kenton, 44
Kenton Mercantile, 45
Kentucky,
Keokuk Falls, 85, 86, 126
Keokuk, Moses, 85
Keota, 206
Keystone Lake, 8
Kiliahote, 30
"Killed with Blunt Arrow," 20
Kincaide, Marlene, 90
King Ferdinand, 10
Kingfisher, 50
Kingfisher County, 62, 63, 64, 95, 119
Kinzer, H. Grant, 145
Kiowa, x, 5, 14, 15, 16, 17, 19, 20, 21, 28, 29, 34, 63, 115, 120, 145, 146, 196, 197
Kiowa Business Committee, 20
Kiowa County, 4, 19, 141, 146, 187

Kiowa County Historical Society, 189
Kirkwood, Herman, 92
Kiwanis Camp Park, 212
Klaus, Doug, 68
Klemme, Robert L. "Bob," 50, 51
Koch, Sheriff Ty, 202
Konawa, 72, 92, 127, 171
Kooie-pah-gaw, 19
Korean War, 147
Kwitny, Jonathan, 201

L

"Lady Desperado, The," 74
"Lafe" Shadley, 53
Laflerie freighting Company, 63
Laird, Jackie McFarland, 56
Lake Altus-Lugert, 4
Lake Eufaula, 214
Lake Humphreys, 99
Lake Tenkiller, 149
Lake Texoma, 156, 157
"Lake Texoma," 156
Lambert, Brother Dominic, 71
Lane, Dan, 152
Langley, Sam, 198
Lapine, Neita, 132
Las Cruces, New Mexico, 145
"Last of the Mohicans, The," 149
Latimer County, 74
Latin, 93
Latta, William, 109, 110
Law, Leon "Red," 147
Lawmen & Outlaws in Oklahoma, 92
Lawton, 124
Leased District of Indian Territory, 42
Leavenworth, Gen. Henry, 49
Lee, Thelma Muskrat, 68
Lee, Robert E., 214
LeFlore, Charles, 107
LeFlore County, 2
Left Hand Spring, 48
LeMay, Alan, 16
Lemmons, Frank, 203, 204
Lemmons, Tom, 203
Lenapah, 90
Lentz, Anna May, 110
Leslie, Harry, 109

Lewis, Dee, 135
Liberal, Kansas, 87
LIFE magazine, 35, 151
Lillie, Gordon W. "Pawnee Bill," 113
Little Boggy, 30
"Little Giant, the," 167
"Little Giant from Little Dixie, the," 167
Little, Hoyt, 180
"Little Kansas," 129
Livesay, Noretta, 77
Lockwood, Mike, 94
Loco, 93, 94
"Loco," 94
Loco Citato, 93
Loco Grocery, 94
Logan County, 9
"Lone Hill," 115
Lone Wolf, 5
Long Beach, California, 169
Longest, Caleb J., 14
Longest, Kenneth, 14
Lookout Peak, 44
Lookout Point, 44
"Lords of the Plains," 15
Los Angeles, California, 169, 210
Lost City, 121, 122
"Lost City Meteorite," 122
Lost City School, 122
"Lottawatta," 214, 215
Lottawatta Road, 214
Louisiana, 12
Louisiana Territory, 15, 19
Loveland, 144
Lovell, Bob, 64
Lowry, Kathy DeLonais, 72
Lowry, Tim, 72
Lt. Col. George A. Custer, 34, 38
Lt. T.B. Wheelock, 4
Lucas, Ike, 36
Lugert, 4

M

MK&T (Katy) Railroad, 69, 168
McAskill, Mike, 66
McCalmont, Ralph, 169
McCasland, Howard, 99
McClain County, 49

McClellan-Kerr Arkansas River
  Navigation System, 40, 82
McClenny, Bart, 66
McCurdy, Elmer, 168, 169
McCurry, Bob, 94
McCurtain County, 26, 165
McDaniel, David, *x*
McEntire, Clark, 107
McEntire, John Wesley, 107
McEntire, Reba, 107, 108
McGee, Tom G., 63
McGeisey, Lincoln, 126
McIntosh County, 111, 151, 211
McIntyre, Glen, *x*
McMichael, Sam, 119
McReynolds, Edwin C., *x*
Madison, 45
Maine, 169
Major County, 59
Major County Historical Society, 60
Mancos, Colorado, 90
Mangum, 83
Mangum, A.S., 83
Mannford, 8
Mankiller, Wilma, 23
Marietta, 210
Marland, 57, 58
Marland Mansion and Estate, 56
Marlboro, commercials, 129
"Marlboro Man," 129
Marlow, 99
Mars, 122
Marsh, Ora, 93
Martin, Billy Dean, 152
Marvin, Lee, 144
Maschino, Pete, 95
Masonic Lodge, 30
Masons, 92
Matthew, Steve, 72
Maud, 134, 135
Maud Housing Authority, 135
"Maud and Bowlegs," 135
Max, 70, 186
Maximilian, 42
Mayfield, Johnny, 193, 194
Maynard, Ken, 56
Mayor Sue Goodnight, 172, 173
Medicine Lodge Treaty, 16

Medicine Spring, 178
Medicine Spring Ranch, 178
Metcalfe, Augusta Corson, 35
Mexican, 88
Mexican-American War, 83
Mexican Emperor Maximilian, 42
"Mexican Joe" Borrero, 56
"Mexican mission brand," 200
"Mexican village," 5
Mexico, 8, 20, 24, 34, 44, 49, 123, 200
Metz, 89
Miami, 105
Michigan,
Middle Boggy, 30
Miles, John D., 63
Miller Brothers 101 Ranch Wild West
  Show, 54
Miller, Col. George Washington, 55, 58
Miller, George L., 55
Miller, 'Deacon Jim," 92
Miller, Joe, 55
Miller, Max, 110
Miller, Zachary Taylor "Zack," 55, 57
Minner, D.C., 152
"Miss Snake Charmer," 117
Mississippi, 26
Mississippi River, 14
Missouri, 8, 97, 105, 115, 137, 152,
  162, 173
Mitchell, Barney, 121, 122
Mix, Tom, 56
Model T Ford, 14, 185
Moeller, Gary, 104
Momaday, N. Scott, 20
Monkey Island, 67
Montana, 19
"Monte Walsh," 144
Montgomery, Janna, 36
Montgomery, Max, 36
"Monty" Roberts, 45
Monument Hill, 57
Moonshine Road, 176, 177
Moore, Gary, 25
Moore, Pat, 141
Morgan, Bill, 79
Morrell, Coeta, 131
Morris, John W., *x*
Morrison, A.J., 126

Morrison, F. Bam, 78, 79
Moscow, 125
Moscow Flats, 125
Motley, Arlis, 102
Mounds, 3
Mountain Fork River, 26
Mountain View, 19, 20, 120, 146
"Mrs. Goombi," 20
Muddy Boggy, 30
Muldrow, 23, 82
Mullendore Cross Bell Ranch, 200
Mullendore, E.C., 201, 202
Mullendore, E.C. III, 200, 201
Mullendore, E.C. "Gene," 200
Mullendore, Erd C., 200
Mullendore, Gene, 200, 201, 202
Mullendore, Kathleen, 200, 201
Mullendore, Linda Vance, 201
"Mullendore Murder Case, The," 201
Murphey, Jerry, 56
Murphy, Mildred, 172
Murphey, Minnie Alemeda, 56
Murray County, 132
Murray, Neil, 53
Muse, Glen, 131
Museum of the Cherokee Strip, x
Museum of the Great Plains, 124
Museum of the Western Prairie, 66
Muskogee, 75
Muskogee County, 151
Muskogee Daily Phoenix & Times-Democrat, The, x
Muskogee Public Library, 25
Mustang, 130, 131
Mustang Creek, 130
Mustang Roundup Club, 131
Mustang Town Center, 130

N

Nall, Hugh "Buck," 112
Napoleon III, 42
National Anthem, 76
National Cowboy & Western Heritage Museum, 107, 151
National Cowgirl Hall of Fame, 35
National Finals Rodeo, 107

National Historic Landmark and Museum, 124
National Register of Historic Places, 35, 57
"Native Americans," 81
Navajo, 15, 16, 18
Navajo Mountain, 15, 16, 17
Navajoe, 15, 16
Nease, Maria, 118
Needmore, 67
Needmore-Bernice, 68
Neill, Jay Wesley, 124
Neosho (District), 24
Neosho River, 24, 67
New Mexico, 8, 15, 123
New Mexico State University, 113, 145
New Mexico Territory, 44, 45
New Spain, 12
New York, 135, 144
Newcomb, Alfred George "Bitter Creek," 53
Newkirk, 10, 57
Newton, Bobby, 207, 212
Nicodemus, Spiro, 2
No Man's Land, 7, 9, 44, 87, 160
No Man's Land Historical Society, 203
No Man's Land Museum, x, 87
"No Wata," 89
Noble County, 57
Nofire, Dennis, 149, 150
Nofire Hollow, 149, 150
Nofire, Sherman, 149, 150
Norman, 80, 81, 99, 112, 169
North Canadian River, 48, 85, 111, 125
North Fork of the Canadian River, 48, 85
North Fork of the Red River, 4, 5, 15, 16, 158
North Texas, 20
Northwest Passage, 203
"Not Your Typical Hooker," 161
Nowata, 89, 90
"NOWATA!," 89
Nowata Chamber of Commerce, 90
Nowata County, 89
Noweta, 89
Nowhere, 216, 217
Nye, W.S., x

O

O.K. Hotel, 53
O'Dell, Larry, x
Ogle, Dr. Charlie, 50
Oglesby, Louella, 210
Ohio, 97, 191
"Oil Patch Mania," 182
Okay, 25
Okarche, 95
"O-KAR-CHEE!," 95
Okeene, 117, 118
Okeene Rattlesnake Hunt, 117
Okesa, 168, 169
"Okie," 1, 148
Oklahoma, x, 2, 4, 5, 7, 8, 9, 10, 12, 13, 14, 15, 16, 18, 19, 20, 22, 23, 24, 26, 27, 28, 30, 32, 33, 34, 35, 37, 38, 40, 42, 46, 48, 49, 50, 52, 53, 54, 56, 58, 61, 64, 65, 66, 67, 69, 71, 73, 74, 76, 78, 79, 80, 82, 83, 88, 89, 91, 92, 93, 95, 97, 99, 101, 103, 105, 107, 109, 111, 113, 115, 117, 119, 121, 122, 123, 124, 125, 126, 128, 130, 132, 134, 136, 138, 143, 145, 146, 149, 151, 152, 154, 156, 157, 160, 162, 165, 167, 170, 172, 174, 176, 178, 179, 180, 182, 183, 185, 187, 190, 191, 193, 194, 195, 196, 197, 200, 202, 205, 207, 209, 210, 212, 214, 217
"Oklahoma," 2
"Oklahoma!," 76
Oklahoma Atlas & Gazetteer, 81
"Oklahoma Blues Hall of Fame," 152
Oklahoma Board on Geographic Names, x, 81
Oklahoma Cattlemen's Association, 202
Oklahoma Cattlemen's Association Range Round-Up, 201
Oklahoma City, 9, 48, 92, 107, 118, 125, 130, 150, 163, 164
Oklahoma Department of Transportation, x
Oklahoma Farm Bureau, 119
Oklahoma Hall of Fame, 35
Oklahoma Historical Society, x, 2, 23, 25, 26, 28, 35, 57, 152
Oklahoma Methodist Manor, 68
Oklahoma Panhandle, 44, 87, 156, 160, 203
"Oklahoma Place Names," x
Oklahoma Senate, 150
Oklahoma State Capitol, 22
Oklahoma State Department of Highways, 214
Oklahoma State University, 113, 161
Oklahoma Station, 76
Oklahoma Territorial Museum, 169
Oklahoma Territory, 4, 7, 9, 16, 19, 42, 53, 63, 69, 76, 91, 95, 102, 109, 110, 113, 115, 116, 119, 122, 123, 125, 126, 130, 136, 141, 143, 146, 154, 156, 158, 160, 162, 168, 172, 176, 200
"Oklahoma's oldest town on Red River," 12
Oklahomans, 1, 65, 215
Oklahoman, The, 188
Okmulgee County, 138
Oktaha, 151, 152, 153
"Old Charlie," 58
Old Day County Reunion, 110
"Old Greer County," 4, 101
"Old Oklahoma," 53, 95
Old Settlers Reunion, 53
"Old Spanish Town," 5
Old West, 1, 48, 52, 113
Ol' Red, 205
Olds, Fred, 169
Olympic Games, 85
"Once a Hooker Always a Hooker," 161
Onco, Atwater, 20
101 Ranch Wild West Show, 113
101 Ranch, 54
101 Ranch Historic District, 57
101 Ranch Old Timers Association, 56
101 Saloon, 58
101 Web site, 58
O'Pry, Carl, 119
O'Pry, Margaret, 119
"179 Friendly People," 173
Onsted, Michigan, 56
Oologah, 103
Oologah Historical Society, 104
Organic Act, 53

Orienta, 59
Osage, 14, 24, 28, 63
Osage County, 168, 191, 200, 202
"Osage, the," 168
Osage Nation, 168
Ottawa County, 105
Otter Creek, 28
Owens, Lorraine, 52

P

"Pack Saddle Creek," 37
Packsaddle, 39
Packsaddle Bar, 38
Packsaddle Bridge, 38
Packsaddle Crossing, 37, 38
Packsaddle Wildlife Management Area, 38
Panhandle, 7, 8, 9, 45, 203
Park Hill, 23
Park, Loyd, 14
Parker, Cynthia Ann, 16
Parker, Isaac "Hanging Judge," 74
Parker, Quanah, 16, 144
Parrilla, Gen. Don Diego Ortiz, 12
Parry, Scott, 39
"Pat Hennessy Celebration," 63
"Pat Hennessy Massacre Re-Enactment," 64
Pat Hennessey Memorial Garden, 63
Patterson, Rich, 39
Paw Paw, 82
Paw Paw Bottom, 82
Pawhuska, 104, 168, 169, 202
"Pawnee Bill" Lillie, 113
Payne County, 52, 113
Peach, Terry, 125
Peacheater Creek, 198
Peacock, Dena, 215
"Pee Wee" Carey, 99
Pennington, Sam, 9
Pennsylvania, 56
Pensacola Dam, 207, 208
Peoria, 105, 106
Peoria and Quapaw reserves, 105
Perkins, 113
Perry, *x*
Perry, Ohio, 172

Pershing, Gen. John J., 55
"Pete" Girdner, 180
Peters, Dorothy Schandorf, 69, 70
Petersburg, 12, 14
Peterson, Dennis, 2
"Petticoat Terror of the Plains," 74
Pewo, Herbie, 197
Pickett, Bill, 57
Pie Flat, 190
"Pilot Hills," 34
Pirsch, Stacey, 129
"Pistol Pete" Eaton, 113
Pittsburg County, 167
Plains Indians, *x*, 4, 34, 42, 122
"Pleasant Hill," 198
Point TV, 169
"Pole Cat Creek," 61
Pole Cat Ranch, 61
Polecat Creek, 61
Polecat Station, 61
Polk, President James, 49
"Polo Estates," 131
Ponca Chief White Eagle, 57
Ponca City, 56, 57, 58
Ponca City Cultural Center, 56
Poncho, 36
Poolaw, Doris, 28
Possum Hollow, 205, 206
"Possum Hollow," 206
"Possum Hollow News," 206
Post, Wiley, 104
Poteete, E.L., 177
Poteete, Erma Renfro, 177
Poteete, Tim, 124
Potrero, El, 88
Pottawatomie and Shawnee lands, 71, 91, 126
Pottawatomie County, 71, 85, 91, 126, 172
Pottawatomie Indians, 72
Prentice, Frank, 40
President James Polk, 49
President Teddy Roosevelt, 123, 144
President Theodore "Teddy" Roosevelt, 55
Principal Chief Chad Smith, 23
Proctor, Ezekiel "Zeke," 32, 33
Protti, Maria, 81

Pueblo, 45
Punkin Ridge, 151, 152, 153
Punkin Ridge Reunion, 152
Pushmataha County, 178
Pussy Cat Nell, 87

Q

Quait, Jack, 57
Quanah, 83
Quapaw, 105
Quartz Mountain Resort Park, 5, 6
Quartz Mountains, 4

R

Ragtown, 182
Rainy Mountain, 19, 20
Rainy Mountain Kiowa Indian Baptist Church, 19
Rainy Mountain School, 19
Ramos, Jeci, 116
Ramos, Raymond, 116
Randlett, 144
Ransom, George, 53
Ransom's Saloon, 53
Ratliff, Wendi, 124
Ravia, 209, 210, 211
"Red Buck" Waightman, 53
Red Fork of the Arkansas River, 8
"Red" Law, 147
"Red People," 76
Red River, 12, 49, 50, 65, 140, 144, 159
Red River Wars, 64
Red Rock Canyon, 212
Red Rock Canyon State Park, 212
Redbird Smith Nighthawk Keetoowah Society, 176
Reed, 84
Reed, Jim, 74
Renbarger, Thom, x
Renfrow, 61
Rentiesville, 151, 152, 153
Republic of Texas, 24
Rev. Allen Wright, 30, 76
Rev. Lucius Aitson, 120
Review, The, 192

Reydon, 35
Reynolds, Virginia, 81
Riggs, Lynn, 76
Rio de los Carneros Cimarron, 8
Rio Grande River, 50
Rio Grande turkeys, 35
Risley, Gene, 177
Ritter, Al, 58
"River of the Wild Sheep," 8
Roach, Ginger, 157
Roan, 69
Robbers Cave, 74, 75
Robbers Cave State Park, 74, 75
Robbers' Roost, 44, 45
Roberts, Monty Joe, 45
Roberts, Vicki, 45
Roberts, William "Monty," 45
Robertson, Louise, 111
Robot, Father Isidore, 71
Rock Creek, 132
Rocky Mountain School, 149
Rocky Mountains, 2
Rockies, 141
Rodgers and Hammerstein, 76
Rodeo Hall of Fame, 107, 151
Roger Mills County, 34, 37, 80, 136, 158, 162, 180, 190
Rogers County, 103
Rogers, Jimmy, 104
Rogers, Tiana, 24
Rogers, Will, 103, 104
Rogers, Will Jr., 104
Roll, 190
Rolston Cemetery, 67
Rolston, Louis Jr., 67
Roman Nose, 154, 155
"Roman Nose brand," 155
"Roman Nose Canyon," 154
Roman Nose, Henry Caruthers, 154
Roman Nose Resort Park, 154
Roman Nose State Resort, 154
"Roman Nose, the History of the Park," 154
Roosevelt, 28, 141, 142
Roosevelt, President Teddy, 144
Roosevelt, President Theodore "Teddy," 55
Route 66, 1

"Rudolph the Red-Nosed Reindeer," 210
Ruth, Kent, x
Russia, 125
Ryan, 14
Ryan Leader, The, 14

S

Sac and Fox, 85
Sac and Fox lands, 85
Sacred Heart, 71, 72
"Sacred Heart Church," 71
Sacred Heart Historical Society, 72
Sacred Heart Mission, 71
Saddle Mountain, 119, 120
Saddle Mountain Indian Mission, 119
"Sailor," 58
Sain-toh-oodle, 20
Saint Louis, 172, 173
"Saint Louis," 172
Sallisaw, 2, 22, 23, 174
Salt Fork of the Arkansas River, 54
Salt Springs, 185, 186
"Sam Jones," 58
Sampson, Palmer, 126
San Bernardo, 12, 14
San Francisco, 145
San Francisco, California, 145
San Francisco Examiner, The, 145
Sanders, Clara, 116
Santa Claus, 187
Santa Fe, New Mexico, 149
Santa Fe Trail, 8, 44
Sayre, 163
Schaefer, Jack, 144
Schandorf, Gene, 70
Schmidt, Darrell, 196
Schmidt, Phyllis, 196
Schreiner, Dr. Terry J., 112
Schreiner, Wanda Lee Crawford, 112
Scotch, 48
Scrudder, Norris, 196
"Searchers, The," 16
Seattle, Washington, 145
Selman, Bob, 186
Selman Ranch, 185
Selman, Sue, 186

Seminole, 14, 34, 126, 134
Seminole County, 134, 170
Seminole Nation, 134, 170
Sequoyah, 22, 23, 49
Sequoyah County, 82, 174, 176
Sequoyah's Cabin, 22
Shadley, Lafayette "Lafe," 53
Shamrock Saloon, 109, 110
Shawnee, 71
Shawnee Cattle Trail, 151
Sheriff George Wayman, 201
Sheriff Ty Koch, 202
Shero, Kay, 75
Shidler, 192
Shirk, George, *x*
Shoaf, Connie, 110
Shoemaker, Edward Connie, *x*
Shoshone, 15
Shultz, Charley, 56
Shumaker, Betty, 97
Sigle, John, 118
"SIMMER ON!" 9
Simmons, Del, 53
Simpsonville, 172, 173
Sims, Bill, 120
"Six Bulls," 24
"Six-Million-Dollar Man," 169
Skin Bayou, 23
Skirdla, Louis, 61
Slapout, 203
Smedley, James "Curbstone Kirby," 57
Smith, J.J., 111
Smith, Maggie, 111
Smith, Principal Chief Chad, 23
Snider, Monte, 115
Snow, Dr. Clyde, 169
Sokoll, Mike, 56
Sooner State, 1, 154, 200
Sorenson, Jack, 36
South American, 97
South Canadian Trail Ride, 110
South Texas, 49
Southern, 34, 40, 82
Southern Cheyenne, 34, 154
"Southern Stage Company," 61
Southwest, 64
Southwest Spanish Mustang Association, 178

"Southwestern Stage Coach Company," 61
Spade Mountain, 183
Spain, 4, 7, 12, 19
Spaniards, 5
Spanish, 1, 4, 8, 10, 12, 13, 15, 36, 93, 97, 170
Spaulding, 193
Spaulding Feed & Supply, 194
Speed, Dick, 53
Spiro, 2, 3
Spiro Mounds, 2
Spiro Mounds Archaeological Center, 2
Spiro Mounds Archaeological State Park, 2
Spivey, Towana, 123
Spook Light Road, 105, 106
Spottedbird, Yale Jr., 16
Spottedhorse, Cornelius, 20
Spradlin, Wayne, 144
St. Gregory's University, 71
"St. Louis," 172, 173
St. Louis Cardinals, 193
Stafford, Cal, 215
Stafford, Carol, 215
"Star Spangled Banner," 107
Starr, Belle, 74, 75
Starr, Blue, 191
Starvation Creek, 158
State Highway 3, 203
State Highway 6, 158
State Highway 8, 118
State Highway 9, 206
State Highway 10, 201
State Highway 28, 207
State Highway 34, 69
State Highway 35, 203
State Highway 39, 71, 127
State Highway 50, 125
State Highway 51, 118, 184
State Highway 54, 28
State Highway 58, 46, 195
State Highway 59, 134
State Highway 82, 176
State Highway 99, 170
State Highway 100, 149
State Highway 101, 23
State Highway 156, 57

State Line Bingo, 88
State Rep. Mark "Buzz" Bradshaw, 38
Stauber, Rose, 67
Staveley Storage, 215
Stearns, Maud, 134
Stephens County, 93, 99
Stephens County Museum, 99
Stewart, Americus, 165
Stewart, Kay, 183
Stewart, Lillian, 183
Stewart, Tom, 165
Stigall, Sam, 57
Stigler, 77, 206
Stigler News-Sentinel, 206
Stiles, Dr. Lewis, 26
Still, Sampson, 177
Stillwater, 89, 161
Stilwell, 149, 183
Stockbridge Mission, 26
Stone, Jim, 208
Stone, Nan, 41
"Story of Ferdinand, The," 11
"Story of Will Rogers, The," 104
Strawberry Springs, 33
Strong City, 180, 181
Strong, Clinton, 180
Stroud, 58
Stubsten, Mark, 60
Studi, Wes, 149
"Sucker Capital of the World," 78
Sucker Day, 79
Sulphur, 132
Summit View Cemetery, 168
Sunday Oklahoman, The, 176
"Support Your Local Hookers," 161
Sutton, David, 212
Sweden, 85
Sweet, Henry, 83, 84
Sweeten, Elvin, 211
Sweeten, Flo, 211
Sweetwater, 158
Swinford, Harry, 119

T

TV, 107, 135, 149, 169, 194
Tabor, Loretta, 179
"Tagonegatty," 20

Tahbone, George, 20
Tahlequah, 22, 33, 149
"Talking Leaves," 22
Tamaha, 40
Taovaya Indians, 12
Tater Hill, 193, 194
"Tater Hill," 194
"Tater Hillbillies, the," 194
Taylor, Dean, 154
Taylor, John, 119
Taylor, Myrna, 97
"Teddy" Roosevelt, 55
Tennessee, 24, 49
Texas, 4, 5, 7, 12, 15, 16, 17, 20, 24, 26, 37, 48, 49, 50, 54, 57, 65, 66, 74, 83, 97, 101, 117, 145, 151, 156, 157, 162, 173, 209
Texas Cavalry, 152
Texas County, 9, 156, 160
"Texas-Oklahoma Colony," 16
Texas Panhandle, 15
Texas Rangers, 34, 37
Texas Road, 30, 151
Texas Road Trading Post and Down Home Blues Club, 151
Texas Trail, 65
Texhoma, 156
Texhoma Auto Supply, 157
Texhoma, Oklahoma, 157
Texokla, 156
Texola, 156
Texoma, 156
Thomas, Gordon, 36
Thompson, Ron, 197
Thorpe, Gail, 85
Thorpe, Grace, 85
Thorpe, Hiram, 85
Thorpe, Jim, 85
"Thoroughbred Acres," 131
Three Forks, 24
Three Forks Treasure Hunters' Club, 25
Threldkeld, John, 160
Threldkeld, Hooker, 161
Threldkeld, "Hooker," 160
Thurman, Marilyn, 148
Tia Juana, 207, 208
"Tia Juana, Oklahoma," 207
Ticky Ridge, 198

Tidwell, Bernice, 162
Tidwell, Chesney, 162
Tidwell, Wilbert, 162, 163, 164
"Tijuana, Mexico," 207
Tillman County, 144
Tin City, 83
Titanic, 183, 184
Titanic Upholstery, 183
To-goam-gatty, 20
Tom, 165
"Tom" Darrigrand, 56
Tom Steed Lake, 141
Tourism and Recreation Department, 169
Traders' Bend Recreation Area, 10
"Tragedy of the Goingsnake District, the," 32
Trail, 69, 70
"Trail of Tears," 14, 32
"Trail of Tears" Drama, 23
Trail Store, 69
Treib, Sharon, 183
Tsain-pope-tday, 20
Tsa-La-Gi Ancient Village, 23
Tsa-Toke, 119
Tucson, Arizona, 20
Tulsa, 68
"Tulsa Jack" Blake, 53
Tunney, Gene, 56
Turley, Gary, 81
Turner, Ken, x
Turpin, 87
TV, 107
2010 Committee, 64

U

U.S., 4, 14, 22, 49, 74, 123, 143, 145
U.S. Army Crops of Engineers, 10
U.S. Board on Geological Names, 80
U.S. Dragoons, 4
U.S. Department of Labor, 145
U.S. General Land Office, 59
U.S. Highway 54, 157
U.S. Highway 59, 174
U.S. Highway 64, 176
U.S. Highway 69, 25
U.S. Highway 81, 48

U.S. Highway 83, 87
U.S. Highway 183, 125, 189
U.S. Highway 281, 48
U.S. Highway 283, 37, 80, 136
U.S. President James Polk, 49
Unassigned Lands, 49, 52, 53, 63, 95
Union, 40, 76, 152
United States, 34
Unkefer, Golda, 73
United States, 24, 42, 49, 123
University of Kentucky, 36
University of Oklahoma, 99
University of Wyoming, 113
Upper Robinson Spring, 109

V

Vamoosa, 170
Vamoosa Baptist Church, 170
Vance, John P., 170
Van Zandt, Sandra, 104
Verden, 42, 43
Verdigris River, 24
Vinson, Bobbie, 75
Violet, 126
Violet Springs, 126, 127
VonGulker, Orville, 117, 118
Vici, 110

W

Waggoner, Mike, 99
Waggoner Ranch, 144
Wagner, Tim, 157
Wagoner County, 24
Wah-Kin-Na, 154
Waightman, George "Red Buck," 53
Waits, Wally, 25
Walker, Francis, 180
Walker, N.A., 53
Wall-Street Journal, The, 201
Ward, Norma Shultz, 56
Warde, Mary Jane, *x*
Warder, Edith, 128
Washington, D.C., 49, 63, 144, 148
Washington state, 207
Washita River, 180

Watson, Louise Michael, 145
Watts, Howard, 82
Wauhillau, 73
Waurika, 14, 50
"Way Down Yonder in the Pawpaw Patch," 82
"Way to Rainy Mountain, The," 20
Wayman, George, 201
Wayman, Sheriff George, 202
Wayne, John, 16
Weatherford, 155
Web site, 152, 160
Webb, Jack, 56, 57, 58
Webber, Desiree, 131
Webbers Falls, 177
Weber, M.C., 154
Weedn, Otto, 116
Welge, Bill, *x*
"Wes Studi Day," 150
West, 200
West Croton Creek, 162
West, Jesse, 92
Western, 144
Western Cherokees, 22, 49
Western Days, 131
Western District of Arkansas, 74
Western History Collections, University of Oklahoma, *x*
Western Trail Historical Society, 65
Westville, 32, 33, 198
Wetumka, 78, 79
Wetzel, Dan, 161
Wheelock, Lt. T.B., 4
"Where the Red Fern Grows," 73
Whisenant, Hugh, 102
Whisenhunt, David, 196
White, ArVel, 161
White Bear, 119
White City, 87
White Eagle, 57
"White Fang Award," 117
White, Larry, 110
"White House, the," 55, 57
Whitebird, Robert, 105
Whitefield, 76, 77
"Whitefield Wal-Mart, the," 77
Whitmire Schoolhouse, 32
Whitson, Shirley, 181

Whittenburg, J.A. "Jim" III, 201
Whittenburg, Katsy Mullendore, 201
Whizbang, 191
Wichita, 2, 4, 10, 12, 13, 14, 42, 48
Wichita and Caddo lands, 46, 143
Wichita, Kansas, 63
Wichita Mountains, 15, 28, 119, 141, 195
Wichita Trace, 48
Wiggins, Jack, 9
Wigwam Neosho, 24, 25
Wilburton, 74, 75, 112
Wild Horse Mountain, 174
Wild Horse Mountain Bar-B-Que, 174
"Wild Horse Park," 131
Wild West, 103
"Wild Woman of the Wild West," 74
Wildcat, 138, 139
Wildcat Junction, 138
Wildman, 141, 142
Wildman, Frank, 141
Will Rogers Memorial Museum, 104
"Will Rogers Story, The," 104
Williams, Bill, 189
Winfield, Darrell, 129
Winkler, Dian, 42
Wirt, 182
Wisconsin, 97
"Witch of Goingsnake and Other Stories, The," 33
"Wizard of Oz, The," 163
Wizzbang, 191, 192
Word, Charles, 110
"Woman Who Stands Behind Tepee," 20
Woods, James, 153
Woods, Ran, 167

Woodward, 37, 70, 186
Woodward, Clarence, 183
Woodward County, 125
Woodward, Pat, 183
Works, Joseph S. "Buckskin Joe," 16
World Championship Cow Chip Throw, 9
World Series, 193
World War II, 3, 119, 165
"World's Greatest Athlete," 85
Wright, Leonard, 157
Wright, Rev. Allen, 30, 76
Wright, Vince, 129
Wyatt, Bobby, 145
Wyatt, Dr. Bob, 145
Wyoming, 15, 35, 129

Y

Yahoo!, 161
Yearwood, Deon, 46
Yellow Snake Saloon, 87
Yellowstone River, 19
York, Donnie, 36
York, Jo Nell, 36
York, John, 152
Younger's Bend, 74
Yukon, 50, 81

Z

"Zack" Miller, 55, 57
"Zeke" Proctor, 32, 33
Zimmerman, Eugene, 195
ZIP code, 157

Other books by Jim Marion Etter:

- Ghost-Town Tales of Oklahoma – Unforgettable Stories of Nearly Forgotten Places
- Thunder in the Heartland – Parables from Oklahoma
- Between Me & You & The Gatepost – Rural Expressions of Oklahoma
- The Grains of Time – A 100-Year Harvest of OGFA Memories
- Oktaha, A Track in the Sand

Etter is also among the authors in anthologies including "Black Hats," edited by Robert J. Randisi; "New Trails," edited by John Jakes and Martin H. Greenberg; "Western Horse Tales," edited by Don Worcester; "Daughters of the Land," edited by Margaret Felt; and "The Salt of the Earth," edited by Bernadette Pruitt.

He has written for magazines including *Persimmon Hill, The Ketchpen, Western Horseman, American Cowboy, Desert Exposure, True West, Frontier Times, Cowboy, Western Digest, Country Discoveries, Route 66, Oklahoma Today* and *ByLine*.

Other books by New Forums Press:

- The Cherokee Strip: Its History and Grand Opening
- Once Upon a Highway: Route 66 in Oklahoma
- Just for Kicks: Oklahoma Route 66 Music Guide
- Oklahoma Cowboy Cartoons
- The Bad Boys of the Cookson Hills
- The Tri-State Terror: The Life and Crimes of Wilbur Underhill
- One Oklahoma Summer
- Stillwater History: The Missing Links
- The Bandit Kings of the Cookson Hills

– and many, many more!

Go to our website at www.newforums.com, or call 1-800-606-3766 for a catalog.

www.ingramcontent.com/pod-product-compliance
Lightning Source LLC
Chambersburg PA
CBHW071154160426
43196CB00011B/2074